Prentice Hall

Biology

Teaching Resources
Unit 3

PEARSON

Prentice
Hall

Upper Saddle River, New Jersey
Boston, Massachusetts

Copyright © by Pearson Education, Inc., publishing as Pearson Prentice Hall, Boston, Massachusetts 02116. All rights reserved. Printed in the United States of America. This publication is protected by copyright, and permission should be obtained from the publisher prior to any prohibited reproduction, storage in a retrieval system, or transmission in any form or by any means, electronic, mechanical, photocopying, recording, or likewise. The publisher hereby grants permission to reproduce these pages, in part or in whole, for classroom use only, the number not to exceed the number of students in each class. Notice of copyright must appear on all copies. For information regarding permission(s), write to: Rights and Permissions Department, One Lake Street, Upper Saddle River, New Jersey 07458.

Pearson Prentice Hall™ is a trademark of Pearson Education, Inc.
Pearson® is a registered trademark of Pearson plc.
Prentice Hall® is a registered trademark of Pearson Education, Inc.

ISBN 0-13-203397-6

1 2 3 4 5 6 7 8 9 10   10 09 08 07 06

To the Teacher

The Teaching Resources unit booklets have been designed to help you teach *Prentice Hall Biology*. Each unit book consists of materials that have been designed to stimulate students' interest in biology, develop their critical thinking, and teach them basic science skills. The unit books will accommodate a wide range of student abilities and interests.

Each teaching resource unit book contains the following:

- Lesson Plans (for each section)
- Reading and Study Workbook A (includes section summaries, section worksheets, and a chapter vocabulary review written at grade level)
- Adapted Reading and Study Workbook B worksheets (Includes section summaries, key concept worksheets, and a chapter vocabulary review written at a sixth-grade reading level)
- Section Review Worksheets
- Enrichment Worksheets
- Graphic Organizers
- Chapter Tests (Includes two tests for each chapter—Test A for students performing on or above grade level; Test B for students performing on or below grade level)
- Unit Tests (two tests for each unit—Test A and Test B)
- Answer Key (for section review worksheets, enrichment worksheets, graphic organizers, and chapter tests.)
- Graphic Organizer Transparencies (generic reproducible masters)
- Transparency Planner (Full-color preview of all the transparencies that support the unit)

Unit 3 Cells
Chapter 7 Cell Structure and Function

Chapter 8 Photosynthesis

Chapter 9 Cellular Respiration

Chapter 10 Cell Growth and Division

LESSON PLAN 7–1 (pages 169–173)

Life Is Cellular

Section Objectives

- **7.1.1 Explain** what the cell theory is.
- **7.1.2 Describe** how researchers explore the living cell.
- **7.1.3 Distinguish** between eukaryotes and prokaryotes.

Vocabulary cell • cell theory • nucleus • eukaryote • prokaryote

Local Standards

1 FOCUS

Reading Strategy
Students make an outline of the section and use the blue heads for the main levels.

Targeted Resources
❑ Transparencies: **93** Section 7–1 Interest Grabber
❑ Transparencies: **94** Section 7–1 Outline

2 INSTRUCT

Build Science Skills: Asking Questions
Students study photos and drawings of cells, label structures, and brainstorm questions about cells. **L1 L2**

Biology and History: Writing Activity
Students research new cell discoveries and present oral reports of their findings to the class. **L2 L3**

Build Science Skills: Classifying
Students classify images as produced by a light microscope, a TEM, an SEM, or a scanning probe microscope. **L2**

Use Visuals: Figure 7–4
Use Figure 7–4 to review the differences between prokaryotic cells and eukaryotic cells. **L1 L2**

Targeted Resources
❑ Reading and Study Workbook: Section 7–1
❑ Adapted Reading and Study Workbook: Section 7–1
❑ Teaching Resources: Section Summaries 7–1, Worksheets 7–1
❑ Transparencies: **95** Prokaryotic and Eukaryotic Cells
❑ **NSTA** *sci*LINKS Cell theory

3 ASSESS

Evaluate Understanding
Ask students to describe how scientists explore living cells and to differentiate between eukaryotes and prokaryotes.

Reteach
Students write statements that apply the ideas of cell theory to specific living things.

Targeted Resources
❑ Teaching Resources: Section Review 7–1
❑ *i*Text Section 7–1

LESSON PLAN 7–2 (pages 174–181)

Eukaryotic Cell Structure

Section Objectives   Local Standards

- **7.2.1 Describe** the function of the cell nucleus.
- **7.2.2 Describe** the functions of the major cell organelles.
- **7.2.3 Identify** the main roles of the cytoskeleton.

Vocabulary organelle • cytoplasm • nuclear envelope
• chromatin • chromosome • nucleolus • ribosome
• endoplasmic reticulum • Golgi apparatus • lysosome • vacuole
• mitochondrion • chloroplast • cytoskeleton • centriole

1 FOCUS

Reading Strategy
Have students preview Figure 7–6 and answer
the caption question.

Targeted Resources
❏ Transparencies: **96** Section 7–2 Interest
Grabber
❏ Transparencies: **97** Section 7–2 Outline
❏ Transparencies: **98** Venn Diagrams

2 INSTRUCT

Build Science Skills: Using Models
Students make a labeled, two-dimensional
model of a typical cell. **L2**

Use Visuals: Figure 7–6
Use Figure 7–6 to introduce students to the
structures of plant and animal cells. **L1 L2**

Use Visuals: Figure 7–7
Use Figure 7–7 to review the structure and
function of the nucleus. **L1 L2**

Build Science Skills: Using Analogies
Ask students to compare a mitochondrion to a
powerhouse. **L2**

Quick Lab
Students make models of cell organelles, and
then the enitre class makes a large model of a
cell. **L2 L3**

Targeted Resources
❏ Reading and Study Workbook: Section 7–2
❏ Adapted Reading and Study Workbook:
Section 7–2
❏ Teaching Resources: Section Summaries 7–2;
Worksheets 7–2
❏ Transparencies: **99** Figure 7–6 Plant and
Animal Cells, **100** Figure 7–11 The
Cytoskeleton
❏ **PHSchool.com** Cell structure

3 ASSESS

Evaluate Understanding
Students make a Venn diagram about structures
found in eukaryotic cells and prokaryotic cells.

Reteach
Students make a compare-and-contrast table
that organizes information about parts of a cell.

Targeted Resources
❏ Teaching Resources: Section Review 7–2
❏ 〈 **iText** 〉 Section 7–2

LESSON PLAN 7–3 (pages 182–189)

Cell Boundaries

Time
3 periods
1 1/2 blocks

Section Objectives

- **7.3.1 Identify** the main functions of the cell membrane and cell wall.
- **7.3.2 Describe** what happens during diffusion.
- **7.3.3 Explain** the processes of osmosis, facilitated diffusion, and active transport.

Vocabulary cell membrane • cell wall • lipid bilayer • concentration • diffusion • equilibrium • osmosis • isotonic • hypertonic • hypotonic • facilitated diffusion • active transport • endocytosis • phagocytosis • pinocytosis • exocytosis

Local Standards

1 FOCUS

Vocabulary Preview
Have students skim the section to identify and make a list of the main ideas.

Targeted Resources
- ❑ Transparencies: **101** Section 7–3 Interest Grabber
- ❑ Transparencies: **102** Section 7–3 Outline

2 INSTRUCT

Use Visuals: Figure 7–12
Use Figure 7–12 to review the structure of a cell membrane. **L1** **L2**

Address Misconceptions
Address the misconceptions that a cell wall takes the place of a cell membrane and a cell wall is impenetrable. **L1**

Demonstration
Demonstrate the concept of selective permeability, using a strainer. **L1** **L2**

Quick Lab
Students investigate a model of permeability in cells. **L2** **L3**

Analyzing Data
Students analyze data in a graph and hypothesize about the relationship between molecule size and rate of diffusion. **L2** **L3**

Targeted Resources
- ❑ Reading and Study Workbook: Section 7–3
- ❑ Adapted Reading and Study Workbook: Section 7–3
- ❑ Teaching Resources: Section Summaries 7–3; Worksheets 7–3
- ❑ Transparencies: **103** Facilitated Diffusion, **104** Figure 7–12 The Structure of the Cell Membrane, **105** Figure 7–15 Osmosis, **106** Figure 7–19 Active Transport
- ❑ Lab Worksheets: Chapter 7 Real-World Lab
- ❑ Lab Manual A: Chapter 7 Lab
- ❑ **NSTA** *SciLINKS* Cell membranes

3 ASSESS

Evaluate Understanding
Challenge students to describe the method a cell would use to transport various substances through the cell membrane.

Reteach
Students compare diffusion, osmosis, facilitated diffusion, and active transport.

Targeted Resources
- ❑ Teaching Resources: Section Review 7–3
- ❑ *iText* Section 7–3

The Diversity of Cellular Life

Time
1 period
1/2 block

Section Objectives

- **7.4.1 Describe** cell specialization.
- **7.4.2 Identify** the organization levels in multicellular organisms.

Vocabulary cell specialization • tissue • organ • organ system

Local Standards

1 FOCUS

Vocabulary Preview
Make a concept map on the board, using the section's Vocabulary words.

Targeted Resources
- ❏ Transparencies: **107** Section 7–4 Interest Grabber
- ❏ Transparencies: **108** Section 7–4 Outline

2 INSTRUCT

Use Visuals: Figure 7–21
Use Figure 7–21 to reinforce the concept of cell specialization. **L1** **L2**

Build Science Skills: Using Analogies
Analogize how cells evolved with how society evolved toward greater specialization. **L2** **L3**

Build Science Skills: Applying Concepts
Students study photos, diagrams, or slides of specialized cells and discuss what makes different cells suited to their functions. **L2**

Build Science Skills: Classifying
Play of game of Name That Cell, Tissue, Organ, or Organ System. **L2**

Targeted Resources
- ❏ Reading and Study Workbook: Section 7–4
- ❏ Adapted Reading and Study Workbook: Section 7–4
- ❏ Transparencies: **109** Levels of Organization
- ❏ Teaching Resources: Section Summaries 7–4, Worksheets 7–4, Enrichment
- ❏ Laboratory Manual B: Chapter 7 Lab
- ❏ **PHSchool.com** Career links

3 ASSESS

Evaluate Understanding
Ask students to explain the levels of organization involved in touch.

Reteach
Students analyze the levels of organization involved in each of the examples shown in Figure 7–21.

Targeted Resources
- ❏ Teaching Resources: Section Review 7–4, Chapter Vocabulary Review, Graphic Organizer, Chapter 7 Tests: Levels A and B
- ❏ *i* **Text** Section 7–4, Chapter 7 Assessment
- ❏ **PHSchool.com** Online Chapter 7 Test

Chapter 7   Cell Structure and Function

Summary

7–1 Life Is Cellular

Since the 1600s, scientists have made many discoveries about the cells of living things. These discoveries are summarized in the cell theory. **The cell theory states:**
- **All living things are made up of cells.**
- **Cells are the basic units of structure and function in living things.**
- **New cells are produced from existing cells.**

All cells share two characteristics:
- a barrier called a cell membrane that surrounds the cell, and
- at some point in their lives they contain DNA. DNA is the molecule that carries biological information.

Cells fall into two broad groups, based on whether they have a nucleus. A **nucleus** is a membrane-enclosed structure that holds the cell's genetic material (DNA). The nucleus controls many of the cell's activities.
- **Prokaryotes** do not have nuclei. **They have genetic material that is not contained in a nucleus.** Bacteria are prokaryotes.
- **Eukaryotes** are cells that have nuclei. **Eukaryotes have a nucleus in which their genetic material is separated from the rest of the cell.** Plants, animals, fungi, and protists are eukaryotes.

7–2 Eukaryotic Cell Structure

Cell biologists divide the eukaryotic cell into two main parts: the nucleus and the cytoplasm. The **cytoplasm** is the part of the cell outside the nucleus.

In the Nucleus
   The nucleus contains most of a cell's DNA. The DNA contains the coded instructions for making proteins and other important molecules.
- The nucleus is surrounded by a double membrane called a **nuclear envelope.**
- Inside the nucleus is granular material called **chromatin.** Chromatin is made up of DNA bound to proteins. When the cell divides, this chromatin condenses into chromosomes. **Chromosomes** are threadlike structures. They contain the genetic information that is passed from one generation of cells to the next.
- Most nuclei also have a small, dense region known as the **nucleolus** where the assembly of ribosomes begins.

In the Cytoplasm

Eukaryotic cells have structures called **organelles** within the cytoplasm.

- **Ribosomes** are small particles of RNA and protein spread throughout the cytoplasm. **Proteins are made on ribosomes.**
- The **endoplasmic reticulum (ER)** is an internal membrane system. **The ER is where lipid components of the cell membrane are assembled, along with proteins and other materials that are exported from the cell.** The part of the ER involved in the protein synthesis is called rough ER. Rough ER has ribosomes on its surface. Smooth ER does not have ribosomes on its surface. Smooth ER helps make lipids.
- **Golgi apparatus** appear as closely grouped membranes. **The job of the Golgi apparatus is to change, sort, and package proteins and other materials from the ER for storage in the cell or secretion outside the cell.**
- **Lysosomes** are small organelles filled with enzymes. Lysosomes help break down lipids, carbohydrates and proteins into small molecules that can be used by the rest of the cell.
- **Vacuoles** are saclike structures that are used to store materials.
- Almost all eukaryotic cells contain **mitochondria. Mitochondria convert the chemical energy stored in food into compounds that are more convenient for the cell to use.**
- Plants and some other organisms contain **chloroplasts. Chloroplasts capture the energy in sunlight and convert it into chemical energy.**
- The structure that helps support the cell is called the **cytoskeleton. The cytoskeleton is a network of protein filaments that helps the cell maintain its shape. The cytoskeleton is also involved in movement.**

7–3 Cell Boundaries

A thin, flexible barrier known as the **cell membrane** surrounds all cells. The makeup of most cell membranes is a double-layered sheet called a lipid bilayer. **The cell membrane**
- **controls what enters and leaves the cell, and**
- **protects and supports the cell.**

Cells of plants, algae, fungi, and many prokaryotes also have a strong supporting layer called a **cell wall** surrounding the cell membrane. **The main job of the cell wall is to support and protect the cell.**

One of the most important functions of the cell membrane is to control the movement of dissolved molecules from the liquid on one side of the membrane to the liquid on the other side.

The cytoplasm of a cell is a solution of many substances in water. Particles in a solution move constantly. Particles tend to move from an area where they are more concentrated to an area where they are less concentrated. This process is called **diffusion. Diffusion does not require energy.**

- Water passes easily across most membranes. **Osmosis is the diffusion of water through a selectively permeable membrane.** A selectively permeable membrane is a membrane that some substances can pass through, while others cannot.

- Many cell membranes have protein channels that let certain molecules cross the membranes. These protein channels facilitate, or help, the diffusion of the molecules across the membrane. This process is called **facilitated diffusion**. It does not require the cell to use energy.

Active transport requires energy. **Active transport** occurs when cells move materials from one side of a membrane to the other side against the concentration difference. Four types of active transport are:

- **endocytosis:** the process of taking material into the cell by means of infolding of the cell membrane

- **phagocytosis:** the extension of cytoplasm to surround a particle and package it within a food vacuole

- **pinocytosis:** the taking up of liquids from the environment

- **exocytosis:** the release of materials from the cell

7–4 The Diversity of Cellular Life

A *unicellular organism* is made up of only one cell. Unicellular organisms carry out all the essential functions of life. Multicellular organisms are made up of many cells. **Cells throughout an organism can develop in different ways to perform different tasks.** This process is called **cell specialization.**

Multicellular organisms have several levels of organization.

- Individual **cells** are the first level.

- Similar cells form units called **tissues.** A tissue is a group of cells that carry out a particular function.

- Groups of tissues that work together form an **organ.**

- A group of organs that work together to perform a specific function is an **organ system.**

Prokaryotic and Eukaryotic Cells

Look at the diagrams below. Label the prokaryotic cell *and the* eukaryotic cell.

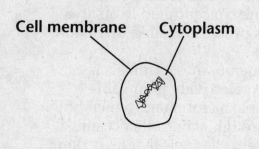

Cell membrane   Cytoplasm

_____

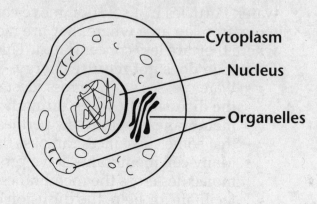

Cytoplasm

Nucleus

Organelles

_____

Use the diagrams to answer the question.

1. Explain why you labeled each diagram as you did.

_____

_____

Compare and contrast the two types of cells by completing the table.

	Prokaryotic Cell	**Eukaryotic Cell**
Cell membrane	present	
Nucleus		present
Cell size		large
Complexity	simple	

Answer the questions. Circle the correct answer.

2. What type of cells makes up your body?

   prokaryotic   eukaryotic

3. What type of cell is a bacterial cell?

   prokaryotic   eukaryotic

Plant Cell

Use the words below to label the plant cell. Some structures have already been labeled for you.

cell wall	mitochondrion	ribosome
chloroplast	nucleus	vacuole

Plant Cell

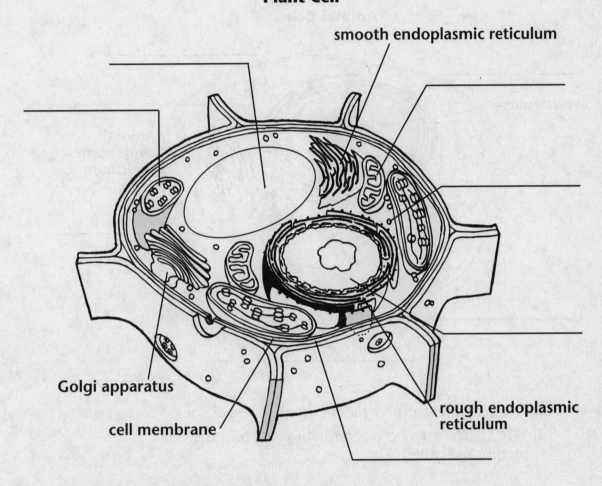

smooth endoplasmic reticulum

Golgi apparatus

cell membrane

rough endoplasmic reticulum

Use the diagram to answer the questions.

1. Which structure is found in a plant cell but not in an animal cell? Circle the correct answer.

chloroplast   cell membrane   ribosome

2. What is the main function of vacuoles?

_____

Animal Cell

Use the words below to label the animal cell. Some structures have already been labeled for you.

cell membrane	mitochondrion	rough endoplasmic reticulum
Golgi apparatus	nucleus	ribosome

Animal Cell

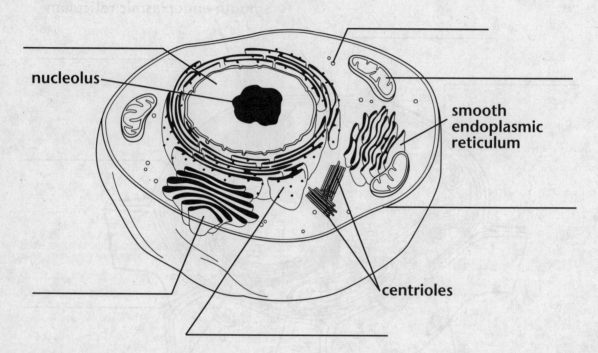

Use the diagram to answer the questions.

1. What is the area between the nucleus and the cell membrane called?

_____

2. What cell structures are found on the surface of rough endoplasmic reticulum but not on smooth endoplasmic reticulum?

_____

Organelle Function

An organelle is a specialized cell structure. Each organelle functions in a different way to help the cell carry out life processes.

A mitochondrion, nucleus, endoplasmic reticulum, and Golgi apparatus *are pictured and described below. Write the name of the organelle underneath its picture.*

Organelle	Function
	controls most cell processes and stores genetic material
	makes membrane lipids that will be exported out of the cell
	modifies, sorts, and packages materials from the endoplasmic reticulum
	converts the energy stored in food into a more useable form

Use the table to answer the question.

1. Which of the structures shown above contains a nucleolus?

_____

Cell Membranes

The cell membrane controls what enters and leaves the cell.
Most cell membranes are made up of a phospholipid bilayer.
This bilayer usually contains membrane proteins embedded in it.

Draw a diagram of a portion of a cell membrane. Label the cytoplasm
and the area outside the cell. *A sample phosolipid and membrane
protein have been diagrammed for you.*

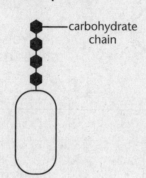

membrane protein

carbohydrate
chain

phospholipid

Answer the question.

1. What do the carbohydrate chains on some membrane
   proteins do?

   _____

   _____

Diffusion and Osmosis

Diffusion is the movement of particles from an area of high concentration to an area of low concentration. Osmosis is the diffusion of water through a selectively permeable membrane.

Look at the beakers on the left. In the beakers on the right, draw in any changes in water level or number of solute particles on each side of the membrane that occur as a result of the described process.

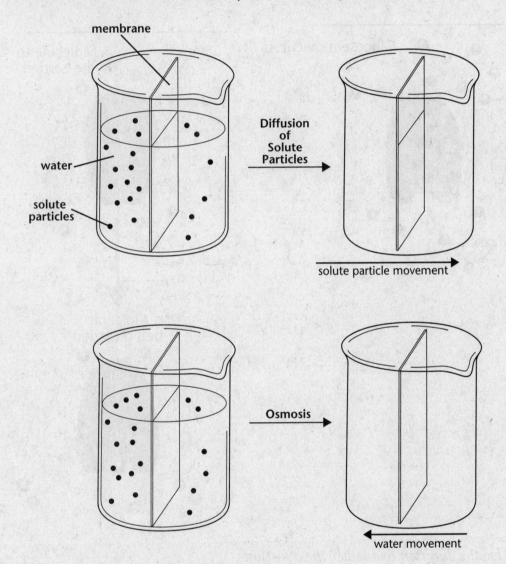

Use the diagrams to answer the question.

1. Look at the top left beaker. What would happen if the membrane did not allow water or solute particles to pass through it?

_____

_____

Facilitated Diffusion and Active Transport

Facilitated diffusion occurs when a substance diffuses across the cell membrane through a protein channel. Active transport occurs when the cell uses energy to carry a substance across the cell membrane.

Look at the diagrams. Label each as either facilitated diffusion *or* active transport.

_____   _____

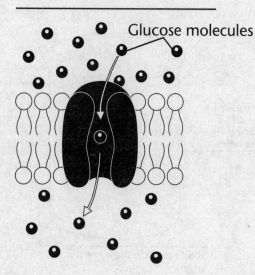

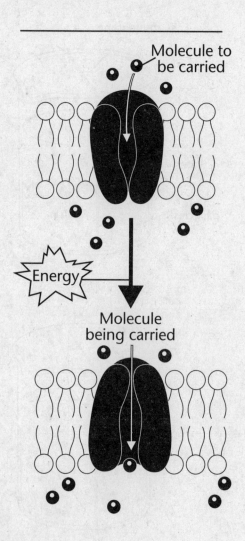

Use the diagram to answer the questions.

1. Which process can move molecules from a lower concentration solution on one side of the membrane to a higher concentration solution on the other side?

_____

2. Which process does not require energy?

_____

Multicellular Organisms—Levels of Organization

The levels of organization in a multicellular organism are cells, tissues, organs, and organ systems.

Draw arrows that show how the levels are organized. Start with the lowest level, and draw an arrow to the next higher level of organization. Continue until you reach the highest level of organization.

Organ system

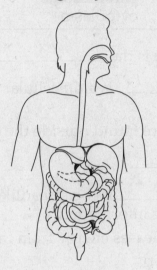

Tissue

Cell

Organ

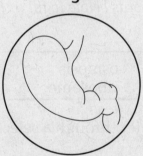

Use the diagram to answer the questions.

1. What is a group of cells that perform a particular function called?

   _____

2. What is a group of tissues that work together called?

   _____

Chapter 7   Cell Structure and Function

Vocabulary Review

Completion   *Use the words below to fill in the blanks with terms from the chapter.*

| cell | chromosome | mitochondrion |
| cell wall | cytoplasm | prokaryote |

1. The basic unit of life is the _____.

2. A _____ is a unicellular organism that lacks a nucleus.

3. The support structure found outside the cell membrane is the

   _____.

4. A _____ is the threadlike nuclear structure that contains genetic information.

5. An organelle that releases energy from food molecules is a

   _____.

6. The material inside the cell membrane that surrounds the

   nucleus is the _____.

Completion   *Use the words below to fill in the blanks with terms from the chapter.*

| nucleus | osmosis | tissue |
| organ | ribosome | |

7. The diffusion of water through a selectively permeable

   membrane is _____.

8. A group of similar cells that work together to perform a

   specific function is called a(an) _____.

9. Proteins are made on a(an) _____.

10. A group of tissues that work together to perform a similar

    function is called a(an) _____.

11. The _____ is the structure in eukaryotic cells that controls cell activities and contains genetic material.

Summary

7–1 Life Is Cellular

Since the 1600s, scientists have made many discoveries that have showed how important cells are in living things. Such discoveries are summarized in the cell theory. The cell theory states:

- All living things are composed of cells.
- Cells are the basic units of structure and function in living things.
- New cells are produced from existing cells.

All cells have two characteristics in common. They are surrounded by a barrier called a cell membrane, and they contain the molecule that carries biological information—DNA.

Cells fall into two broad categories, depending on whether they contain a nucleus. The nucleus is a large membrane-enclosed structure that contains the cell's genetic material in the form of DNA. The nucleus controls many of the cell's activities. Prokaryotic cells have genetic material that is not contained in a nucleus. Bacteria are prokaryotes. Eukaryotic cells contain a nucleus in which their genetic material is separated from the rest of the cell. Plants, animals, fungi, and protists are eukaryotes.

7–2 Eukaryotic Cell Structure

Cell biologists divide the eukaryotic cell into two major parts: the nucleus and the cytoplasm. The cytoplasm is the portion of the cell outside the nucleus. Eukaryotic cells contain structures known as organelles.

The nucleus contains nearly all the cell's DNA and with it the coded instructions for making proteins. The nucleus is surrounded by a nuclear envelope composed of two membranes. Inside the nucleus is granular material called chromatin. Most nuclei also contain a small, dense region known as the nucleolus.

Ribosomes are small particles of RNA and protein found throughout the cytoplasm. Proteins are assembled on ribosomes. Eukaryotic cells contain an internal membrane system known as the endoplasmic reticulum, or ER. The ER is where lipid components of the cell membrane are assembled, along with proteins and other materials that are exported from the cell. The portion of the ER involved in the synthesis of proteins is called rough ER. Smooth ER, which does not contain ribosomes, is involved in the making of lipids. The function of the Golgi apparatus is to modify, sort, and package proteins and other materials from the ER for storage in the cell or secretion outside the cell.

Other organelles include lysosomes, vacuoles, mitochondria, and chloroplasts. Mitochondria are organelles that convert the chemical energy stored in food into compounds that are more convenient for the cell to use. Chloroplasts are organelles that capture the energy from sunlight and convert it into chemical energy.

Eukaryotic cells have a structure called the cytoskeleton that helps support the cell. The cytoskeleton is a network of protein filaments that helps the cell to maintain its shape. The cytoskeleton is also involved in movement.

7–3 Cell Boundaries

All cells are surrounded by a thin, flexible barrier known as the cell membrane. The cell membrane regulates what enters and leaves the cell and also provides protection and support. The composition of nearly all cell membranes is a double-layered sheet called a lipid bilayer. Many cells also produce a strong supporting layer around the membrane known as the cell wall. Cell walls are present in plants, algae, fungi, and many prokaryotes. The main function of the cell wall is to provide support and protection for the cell.

One of the most important functions of the cell membrane is to regulate the movement of dissolved molecules from the liquid on one side of the membrane to the liquid on the other side. The cytoplasm of a cell contains a solution of many different substances in water. The concentration of a solution is the mass of solute in a given volume of solution.

In a solution, particles move constantly. Particles tend to move from an area where they are more concentrated to an area where they are less concentrated, a process called diffusion. When the concentration of a solute is the same throughout a solution, the solution has reached equilibrium. Because diffusion depends upon random particle movements, substances diffuse across membranes without requiring the cell to use energy. Water passes quite easily across most membranes. Osmosis is the diffusion of water through a selectively permeable membrane. Many cell membranes have protein channels that allow certain molecules to cross the membranes. In such cases, the cell membrane protein is said to facilitate, or help, the diffusion of the molecules across the membrane. This process is called facilitated diffusion. It does not require use of the cell's energy.

Active transport does require the cell's energy. In active transport, cells move materials from one side of a membrane to the other side against the concentration difference. Types of active transport include endocytosis, phagocytosis, pinocytosis, and exocytosis.

7–4 The Diversity of Cellular Life

An organism that consists of a single cell is called a unicellular organism. Unicellular organisms carry out all the essential functions of life. Organisms that are made up of many cells are called multicellular organisms. Cells throughout a multicellular organism can develop in different ways to perform different tasks. This process is called cell specialization.

The levels of organization in a multicellular organism are individual cells, tissues, organs, and organ systems. Individual cells are the first level. Similar cells are grouped into units called tissues. A tissue is a group of cells that perform a particular function. Groups of tissues that work together form an organ. A group of organs that work together to perform a specific function is called an organ system.

Section 7–1 Life Is Cellular (pages 169–173)

👄 **Key Concepts**
- What is the cell theory?
- What are the characteristics of prokaryotes and eukaryotes?

Introduction (page 169)

1. What is the structure that makes up every living thing? _____

The Discovery of the Cell (pages 169–170)

2. What was Anton van Leeuwenhoek one of the first to see in the 1600s? _____

_____

_____

3. What did a thin slice of cork seem like to Robert Hooke when he observed it

through a microscope? _____

_____

4. What did the German botanist Matthias Schleiden conclude? _____

_____

_____

5. What did the German biologist Theodor Schwann conclude? _____

_____

_____

6. How did Rudolph Virchow summarize his years of work? _____

_____

_____

7. What are the three concepts that make up the cell theory?

    a. _____

    b. _____

    c. _____

Exploring the Cell (pages 170–172)

8. Why are electron microscopes capable of revealing details much smaller than those

seen through light microscopes? _____

_____

_____

Prokaryotes and Eukaryotes (pages 172–173)

9. Circle the letter of each sentence that is true about prokaryotes.

    a. They grow and reproduce.

    b. Many are large, multicellular organisms.

    c. They are more complex than cells of eukaryotes.

    d. They have cell membranes and cytoplasm.

10. Are all eukaryotes large, multicellular organisms? _____

_____

_____

11. Complete the table about the two categories of cells.

TWO CATEGORIES OF CELLS

Category	Definition	Examples
	Organisms whose cells lack nuclei	
	Organisms whose cells contain nuclei	

Section 7–2 Eukaryotic Cell Structure
(pages 174–181)

Key Concept

- What are the functions of the major cell structures?

Comparing a Cell to a Factory (page 174)

1. What is an organelle? _____

_____

2. Label the structures on the illustrations of the plant and animal cells.

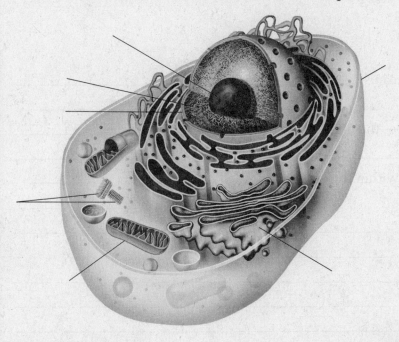

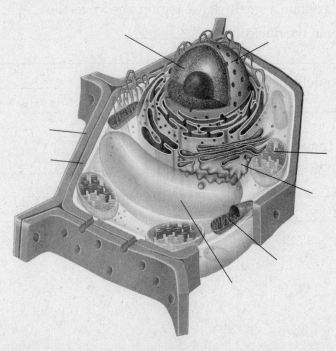

3. Circle the letter of each structure that animal cells contain.

   a. chloroplasts

   b. lysosomes

   c. mitochondria

   d. ER

4. Circle the letter of each structure that plant cells contain.

   a. cell wall

   b. ER

   c. lysosomes

   d. chloroplast

Nucleus (page 176)

5. What is the function of the nucleus? _____
_____

6. What important molecules does the nucleus contain? _____
_____

7. The granular material visible within the nucleus is called _____.

8. What does chromatin consist of? _____
_____

9. What are chromosomes? _____
_____
_____
_____

10. Most nuclei contain a small, dense region known as the _____.

11. What occurs in the nucleolus? _____
_____

12. What is the nuclear envelope? _____
_____

Ribosomes (page 177)

13. What are ribosomes? _____
_____
_____

Endoplasmic Reticulum (pages 177–178)

14. What is the difference between rough ER and smooth ER? _____

_____

_____

Golgi Apparatus (page 178)

15. Using the cell as a factory analogy, describe the role of the Golgi apparatus in the cell.

_____

_____

_____

Lysosomes (page 179)

16. Circle the letter of each sentence that is true about lysosomes.

   a. They contain enzymes that help synthesize lipids.

   b. They break down organelles that have outlived their usefulness.

   c. They produce proteins that are modified by the ER.

   d. They contain enzymes that break down lipids, carbohydrates, and proteins.

Vacuoles (page 179)

17. What are vacuoles? _____

_____

_____

18. What is the role of the central vacuole in plants? _____

_____

_____

19. How does the contractile vacuole in a paramecium help maintain homeostasis?

_____

_____

Mitochondria and Chloroplasts (pages 179–180)

20. Is the following sentence true or false? Both chloroplasts and mitochondria are

   enclosed by two membranes. ——————————————

21. Chloroplasts and mitochondria contain their own genetic information in the form of

_____ .

22. What are mitochondria? _____

_____

_____

23. Are mitochondria found in plant cells, animal cells, or both? _____

24. Where are chloroplasts found? _____

_____

25. Biologist Lynn Margulis has suggested that mitochondria and chloroplasts are descendants of what kind of organisms? _____

_____

Cytoskeleton (page 181)

26. What is the cytoskeleton? _____

_____

_____

27. Complete the table about structures that make up the cytoskeleton.

STRUCTURES OF THE CYTOSKELETON

Structure	Description	Functions
		Maintain cell shape, help build cilia and flagella, form centrioles in cell division
		Support the cell, help cells move

Match the organelle with its description.

Organelle	Description
_____ **28.** Ribosome	**a.** Uses energy from sunlight to make energy-rich food
_____ **29.** Endoplasmic reticulum	
_____ **30.** Golgi apparatus	**b.** Stack of membranes in which enzymes attach carbohydrates and lipids to proteins
_____ **31.** Lysosome	
_____ **32.** Vacuole	**c.** Uses energy from food to make high-energy compounds
_____ **33.** Chloroplast	
_____ **34.** Mitochondrion	**d.** An internal membrane system in which components of cell membrane and some proteins are constructed

e. Saclike structure that stores materials

f. Small particle of RNA and protein that produces protein following instructions from nucleus

g. Filled with enzymes used to break down food into particles that can be used

Reading Skill Practice

A flowchart can help you remember the order in which events occur. On a separate sheet of paper, create a flowchart that describes how proteins are made in the cell. You will find that the steps of this process are explained on pages 176–178. For more information about flowcharts, see Organizing Information in Appendix A in your textbook.

Section 7–3 Cell Boundaries (pages 182–189)

🔑 Key Concepts
- What are the main functions of the cell membrane and the cell wall?
- What happens during diffusion?
- What is osmosis?

Cell Membrane (page 182)

1. What are the functions of the cell membrane? _____
   _____

2. The core of nearly all cell membranes is a double-layered sheet called a(an)
   _____.

3. What is the difference in the function of the proteins and the carbohydrates attached to
   a cell membrane? _____
   _____
   _____

Cell Walls (page 183)

4. In what organisms are cell walls found? _____
   _____

5. Is the following sentence true or false? The cell wall lies inside the cell membrane.
   _____

6. What is the main function of the cell wall? _____
   _____

7. What are plant cell walls mostly made of? _____
   _____

Diffusion Through Cell Boundaries (pages 183–184)

8. What is the concentration of a solution? _____
   _____

9. What is diffusion? _____
   _____

10. What is meant when a system has reached equilibrium? _____
    _____
    _____

11. The molecules of solute in the illustration are moving through the cell membrane from top to bottom. Indicate with labels which side of the membrane has a high concentration of solute and which has a low concentration.

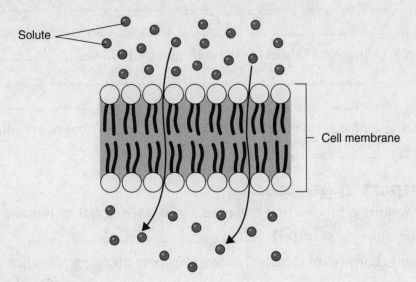

Solute

Cell membrane

Osmosis (pages 185–186)

12. What does it mean that biological membranes are selectively permeable?

_____

_____

13. What is osmosis? _____

_____

14. Is the following sentence true or false? Water tends to diffuse from a region where it is less concentrated to a region where it is highly concentrated. _____

15. When will water stop moving across a membrane? _____

_____

_____

Match the situation to the description.

Situation	Description
_____ **16.** Two solutions are isotonic.	**a.** The solution is above strength in solute.
_____ **17.** A solution is hypertonic.	**b.** The solutions are the same strength.
_____ **18.** A solution is hypotonic.	**c.** The solution is below strength in solute.

19. On which side of a selectively permeable membrane does osmosis exert a pressure?

_____

_____

Facilitated Diffusion (page 187)

20. What happens during the process of facilitated diffusion? _____
_____
_____

21. What is the role of protein channels in the cell membrane? _____
_____
_____

22. Is the following sentence true or false? Facilitated diffusion does not require the cell to use energy. _____

Active Transport (pages 188–189)

23. The energy-requiring process that moves material across a cell membrane against a concentration difference is called _____.

24. Is the following sentence true or false? Active transport always requires transport proteins during the process. _____

25. Complete the table about the types of active transport.

TYPES OF ACTIVE TRANSPORT

Type	Description
Endocytosis	
Phagocytosis	
Exocytosis	

26. During endocytosis, what happens to the pocket in the cell membrane when it breaks loose from the membrane? _____
_____

Section 7–4 The Diversity of Cellular Life
(pages 190–193)

👄 **Key Concepts**

- What is cell specialization?
- What are the four levels of organization in multicellular organisms?

Unicellular Organisms (page 190)

1. A single-celled organism is also called a(an) _____ organism.

Multicellular Organisms (pages 190–192)

2. What is cell specialization in a multicellular organism? _____

_____

_____

3. Circle the letter of each sentence that is true about cell specialization.

   a. Specialized cells perform particular functions within the organism.

   b. Only unicellular organisms have specialized cells.

   c. The human body contains many different cell types.

   d. Some cells are specialized to enable movement.

Levels of Organization (pages 192–193)

4. What are four levels of organization in a multicellular organism?

   a. _____

   b. _____

   c. _____

   d. _____

5. What is a tissue? _____

_____

6. What are the four main types of tissue in most animals?

   a. _____

   b. _____

   c. _____

   d. _____

7. Groups of tissues that work together to perform a specific function are called a(an)

   _____.

8. What kinds of tissues can be found within a muscle in your body? _____

_____

_____

9. What is an organ system? _____

_____

Vocabulary Review

Matching   *In the space provided, write the letter of the function that best matches each organelle.*

_____ **1.** mitochondrion

_____ **2.** ribosome

_____ **3.** endoplasmic reticulum

_____ **4.** Golgi apparatus

_____ **5.** lysosome

_____ **6.** chloroplast

a. site where lipid components of the cell membrane are assembled

b. captures energy from sunlight and converts it into chemical energy

c. modifies, sorts, and packages proteins

d. site where proteins are assembled

e. converts chemical energy in food into compounds the cell can use

f. acts as the cell's cleanup crew

Completion   *Fill in the blanks with terms from Chapter 7.*

7. Bacteria are examples of _____.

8. Cells that are larger and more complex than prokaryotes are _____ cells.

9. The _____ is the portion of the cell outside of the nucleus.

10. The supporting structure of the cell that is also involved in movement is the _____.

11. All cells are surrounded by a flexible barrier known as the _____.

12. The movement of particles from an area of greater concentration to an area of lower concentration is called _____.

13. When comparing two solutions, the solution with the greater concentration of solutes is called _____, while the solution with the lower concentration of solutes is called _____.

14. The process of taking material into the cell by means of infoldings of the cell membrane is called _____.

15. Amoebas use the process of _____ to take in food and other materials.

16. _____ is the process by which cells in an organization develop in different ways to perform different tasks.

17. In the process of _____, a protein channel helps the diffusion of glucose across a membrane.

18. The diffusion of water through a selectively permeable membrane is called _____.

19. The process that moves materials through a membrane against a concentration difference is known as _____.

Chapter 7 Cell Structure and Function   **Section Review 7-1**

Reviewing Key Concepts

Completion *On the lines provided, complete the following sentences.*

1. All _____ are composed of cells.

2. Cells are the basic units of _____ and
   _____ in all organisms.

3. New cells are produced from _____.

4. The cells of eukaryotes have a(an) _____; the
   cells of _____ do not.

5. Eukaryotic cells also have a variety of specialized structures called
   _____.

Reviewing Key Skills

Classifying *On the lines provided, label each cell as either* prokaryotic *or* eukaryotic.

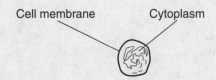

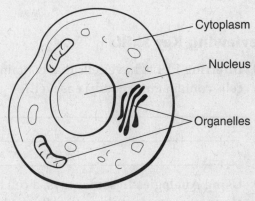

6. _____   7. _____

8. **Calculating** The smallest bacterium is 0.2 micrometers across, while the giant amoeba *Chaos chaos* is 1000 micrometers across. How many times larger is the giant amoeba than the smallest bacterium?

_____

9. **Comparing and Contrasting** Explain the similarities and differences between a prokaryotic cell and a eukaryotic cell.

_____

_____

_____

10. **Applying Concepts** Are human cells prokaryotic or eukaryotic? Explain your answer.

_____

_____

Reviewing Key Concepts

Matching *On the lines provided, match the structure with its function in the cell.*

_____ 1. cell wall

_____ 2. nucleus

_____ 3. cytoskeleton

_____ 4. endoplasmic reticulum

_____ 5. Golgi apparatus

_____ 6. chloroplast

_____ 7. mitochondrion

a. controls most cell processes and contains DNA

b. uses energy from food to make high-energy compounds

c. provides support and protection for the cell

d. maintains cell shape with a network of protein filaments

e. uses energy from sunlight to make food molecules

f. site where lipid components of the cell membrane are assembled and where proteins are chemically modified

g. modifies, sorts, and packages proteins and other materials from the ER

Reviewing Key Skills

8. **Inferring** Plants have cells that contain chloroplasts. Why must their cells contain mitochondria as well?

   _____

   _____

   _____

9. **Using Analogies** In some ways, a cell is analogous to a factory. Create an analogy describing the job of a lysosome within a cellular "factory."

   _____

   _____

   _____

10. **Comparing and Contrasting** What structures make plant and animal cells different?

    _____

    _____

    _____

    _____

Name_____ Class_____ Date _____

Reviewing Key Concepts

Short Answer *On the lines provided, answer the following questions.*

1. What are two functions of the cell membrane?

_____

_____

_____

2. What happens to a higher concentration of dissolved molecules on
   one side of a cell membrane during the process of diffusion?

_____

_____

3. What is osmosis?

_____

_____

_____

Completion *On the lines provided, complete the following sentences.*

4. During the process of _____, a molecule such as
   glucose must use a protein channel to cross through a cell membrane.

5. For a molecule to move from an area of low concentration to high

   concentration, the process of _____ must occur.

Reviewing Key Skills

Interpreting Graphics *On the lines provided, identify each diagram as showing an* isotonic, *a*
hypotonic, or a hypertonic *solution inside the cell and describe how the concentration of water*
molecules will affect the shape of the cell.

6. _____

_____

_____

_____

7. _____

_____

_____

_____

8. _____

_____

_____

_____

Chapter 7 Cell Structure and Function   Section Review 7-4

Reviewing Key Concepts

Short Answer *On the lines provided, answer the following questions.*

1. Why do multicellular organisms contain specialized cells?

   _____

   _____

2. Give two examples of specialized cells and explain the cell's unique
   role in the human body.

   _____

   _____

Identifying Structures *On the lines provided, place the following terms in
order from smallest to largest level of organization.*

_____ 3. tissues

_____ 4. organ systems

_____ 5. organs

_____ 6. individual cells

Reviewing Key Skills

7. **Comparing and Contrasting** Compare the activities of a specialized
   cell in a multicellular organism to those of a unicellular organism.

   _____

   _____

   _____

8. **Using Analogies** The specialized cells in a multicellular organism
   have unique roles to play. Create an analogy that describes a
   situation in which specific organisms or objects have unique roles in
   a system.

   _____

   _____

   _____

9. **Applying Concepts** Is your tongue a tissue, an organ, or an organ
   system? Explain your answer.

   _____

   _____

   _____

10. **Comparing and Contrasting** How are tissues and organs different?

    _____

    _____

    _____

Chapter 7 Cell Structure and Function   Chapter Vocabulary Review

Matching *On the lines provided, match the term with its definition.*

_____ 1. cell

_____ 2. cell membrane

_____ 3. cell wall

_____ 4. nucleus

_____ 5. cytoplasm

_____ 6. prokaryote

_____ 7. eukaryote

_____ 8. organelle

_____ 9. chromatin

_____ 10. phagocytosis

a. organism whose cells contain a nucleus

b. granular material visible within the nucleus

c. the basic unit of life

d. specialized structures within a cell that perform important cell functions

e. organism whose cells do not contain a nucleus

f. strong supporting layer around the cell membrane that protects the cell

g. process by which extensions of cytoplasm engulf large particles

h. large structure that contains the cell's genetic information

i. thin, flexible barrier around the cell

j. portion of the cell outside the nucleus

Multiple Choice *On the lines provided, write the letter that best completes the sentence or answers the question.*

_____ 11. The small dense region in the nucleus where the assembly of ribosomes begins is called the
    a. nucleolus.   b. nuclear envelope.
    c. chloroplast.   d. vacuole.

_____ 12. The network of protein filaments that help maintain the shape of the cell is called the
    a. nucleus.   b. mitochondrion.
    c. cytoskeleton.   d. ribosomes.

_____ 13. Which organelles can use energy from sunlight to create energy-rich food molecules?
    a. lysosomes   b. Golgi apparati
    c. vacuoles   d. chloropasts

_____ 14. What is the process by which material is taken into the cell by infoldings of the cell membrane?
    a. diffusion   b. endocytosis
    c. osmosis   d. exocytosis

_____ 15. The fourth, and highest, level of organization in a multicellular organism is
    a. cell specialization.   b. a tissue.
    c. an organ system.   d. an organ.

Name_____ Class_____ Date _____

Labeling Diagrams *On the lines provided, label the structures found in an animal cell that correspond with the numbers in the diagram.*

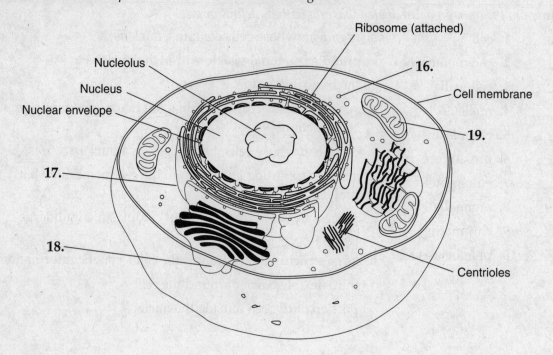

16. _____

17. _____

18. _____

19. _____

Completion *On the lines provided, complete the following sentences.*

20. The distinct, threadlike structures that contain the genetic information of the cell are called _____.

21. Particles tend to move from an area of high concentration to an area of low concentration in a process known as _____.

22. The double-layered sheet that makes up nearly all cell membranes is called the _____.

23. The process in which water diffuses through a selectively permeable membrane is called _____.

24. The process by which a protein channel allows molecules to cross the cell membrane is called _____.

25. The process that requires an input of energy to help material move from an area of lower concentration to an area of greater concentration is called _____.

Chapter 7 Cell Structure and Function   Enrichment

Cell Specialization

As an organism develops, it changes shape and organization. Cells begin to differentiate and form specialized regions of the body. This process of differentiation is called *morphogenesis*. Morphogenesis involves many different processes. For example, some cells split, fold, or bend. Others migrate or combine to form masses, cords, and sheets. Some areas grow faster than other areas.

A second kind of differentiation during growth involves changes in cell structure and development. This process, called *histogenesis*, is the development of different tissues.

A fertilized egg, or zygote, contains all the instructions needed for growth and development. These instructions, stored in the chromosomes, are decoded during histogenesis. At first, all the cells that develop by division of the zygote have the same shape and chemical makeup. Once histogenesis begins, the cells change chemically. Each cell becomes a special type with a unique function.

At the end of the histogenic process, the organism has created the tissues and organs it will need to live. Each organ or type of tissue is formed from a group of cells that have a similar structure and function. The four main types of tissue are the epithelial tissue, connective tissue (including cartilage and bone), muscular tissue, and nervous tissue.

Epithelial tissue is formed by sheets of cells that act as a lining or covering inside or outside the body. For example, your skin is composed of epithelial cells.

Connective tissue is formed by cells that are joined together with fluid, semifluid, or solid substances. Your heart and lungs are surrounded by connective tissue. Cartilage is made up of cells in a matrix and is strengthened by connective issue fibers. Many of your bones are capped in cartilage. Bone is the material that supports your skeletal structure. Bone contains solid material, and there are many types of bones.

Muscular tissue is composed of specialized cells that contract in response to stimuli. Individual muscle fibers can be as long as several centimeters.

Nervous tissue is made of nerve cells that consist of cell bodies and fibers. Nervous tissue coordinates the body by transmitting messages from all its parts to and from the brain.

Evaluation *On the lines provided, answer the following questions.*

1. Compare and contrast morphogenesis and histogenesis.

   _____

   _____

   _____

   _____

2. Where in the zygote's cells are the instructions required for histogenesis stored?

   _____

   _____

Concept Map

Using information from the chapter, complete the concept map below. If there is not enough room in the concept map to write your answers, write them on a separate sheet of paper.

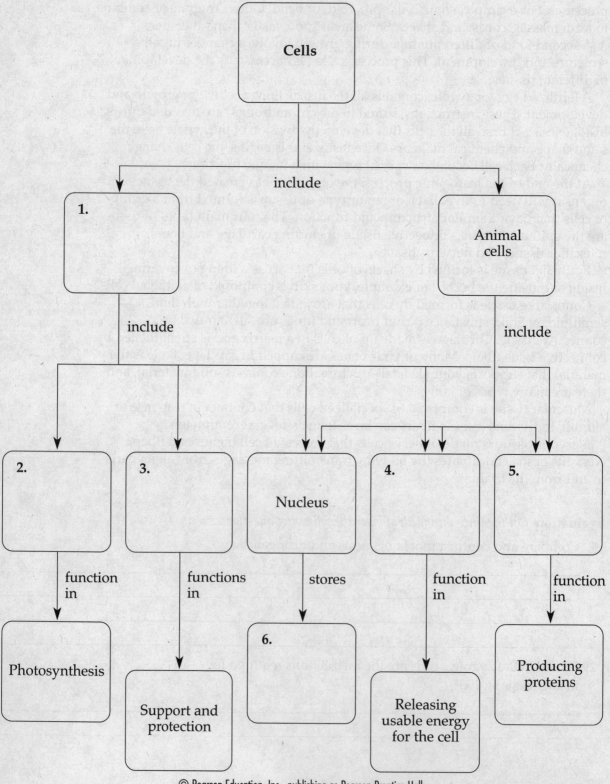

Multiple Choice

Write the letter that best answers the question or completes the statement on the line provided.

_____ 1. The work of Schleiden and Schwann can be summarized by saying that
   a. all plants are made of cells.
   b. all animals are made of cells.
   c. plants and animals have specialized cells.
   d. all plants and animals are made of cells.

_____ 2. Which cell structure contains the cell's genetic material and controls many of the cell's activities?
   a. organelle   c. cell envelope
   b. nucleus   d. cytoplasm

_____ 3. Cells fall into two broad categories, depending on whether they
   a. have a cell wall.
   b. contain genetic material.
   c. have a nucleus.
   d. contain chloroplasts.

_____ 4. Eukaryotes usually contain
   a. a nucleus.
   b. specialized organelles.
   c. genetic material.
   d. all of the above

_____ 5. Which of the following is NOT found in the nucleus?
   a. cytoplasm   c. chromatin
   b. nucleolus   d. DNA

_____ 6. Which structures carry out cell movement?
   a. cytoplasm and ribosomes
   b. nucleolus and nucleus
   c. microtubules and microfilaments
   d. chromosomes

_____ 7. Which organelle breaks down lipids, carbohydrates, and proteins into small molecules that the cell can use?
   a. Golgi apparatus   c. endoplasmic reticulum
   b. lysosome   d. mitochondrion

_____ 8. Which organelle makes proteins using coded instructions that come from the nucleus?

a. Golgi apparatus   c. vacuole

b. mitochondrion   d. ribosome

_____ 9. Which organelle converts the chemical energy stored in food into compounds that are more convenient for the cell to use?

a. chloroplast   c. endoplasmic reticulum

b. Golgi apparatus   d. mitochondrion

_____10. Which of the following is a function of the cell membrane?

a. breaks down lipids, carbohydrates, and proteins from foods

b. stores water, salt, proteins, and carbohydrates

c. keeps the cell wall in place

d. regulates which materials enter and leave the cell

_____11. Diffusion occurs because

a. molecules constantly move and collide with one another.

b. the concentration of a solution is never the same throughout a solution.

c. the concentration of a solution is always the same throughout a solution.

d. molecules never move or collide with one another.

_____12. An animal cell that is surrounded by fresh water will burst because the osmotic pressure causes

a. water to move into the cell.

b. water to move out of the cell.

c. solutes to move into the cell.

d. solutes to move out of the cell.

_____13. The cells of multicellular organisms are

a. smaller than those of unicellular organisms.

b. simpler than those of unicellular organisms.

c. specialized to perform particular functions.

d. not dependent on one another.

_____14. Which of the following is an organ of the digestive system?

a. stomach   c. muscle cell

b. nervous tissue   d. epithelial tissue

_____15. An organ system is a group of organs that

a. are made up of similar cells.

b. are made up of similar tissues.

c. work together to perform a specific function.

d. work together to perform all the functions in a multicellular organism.

Name_____ Class_____ Date _____

Completion

Complete each statement on the line provided.

16. According to the cell theory, new cells are produced from existing _____ .

17. In a eukaryote, the portion of the cell outside the nucleus is called the _____ .

18. During cell division, chromatin condenses to form _____ , which are threadlike structures containing genetic information.

19. Unlike smooth endoplasmic reticulum, rough endoplasmic reticulum has _____ attached to it.

20. The cell takes in food and water and eliminates wastes through the _____ .

Short Answer

In complete sentences, write the answers to the questions on the lines provided.

21. How do prokaryotes and eukaryotes differ?

_____

_____

22. Using Figure 1, give the letter of the structure in diagram II that corresponds to structure H in diagram I. Name the structure and state what process occurs in it.

_____

_____

_____

23. Using Figure 1, give the label letters and full names of two structures that are found in a plant cell but not in an animal cell. State the function of each of these structures.

_____

_____

_____

_____

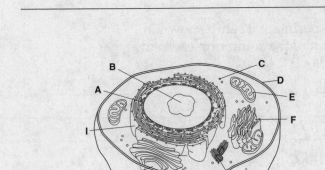

Figure 1

Diagram I

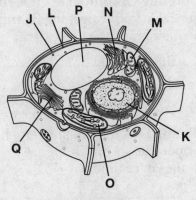

Diagram II

24. Define diffusion.

_____

_____

_____

_____

25. A hypertonic salt solution has a higher concentration of solutes than a blood cell. Explain what happens when a blood cell is placed in a hypertonic salt solution.

_____

_____

_____

Using Science Skills

Use the diagram below to answer the following questions on the lines provided.

A student put together the experimental setup shown below. The selectively permeable membrane is permeable to both types of solute molecules shown.

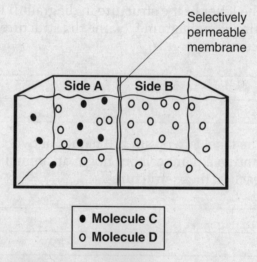

Figure 2

26. Interpreting Graphics Describe the experimental setup shown in Figure 2. Do you expect the distribution of the solutes on each side of the membrane to change over time?

_____

_____

_____

27. Predicting Describe the movement of the C molecules on side A of the apparatus shown in Figure 2. What will happen to these molecules over time?

_____

_____

28. **Predicting** Look at Figure 2. Describe the movement of the D molecules on side A. What will happen to these molecules over time?

   _____

   _____

   _____

29. **Predicting** What will the apparatus shown in Figure 2 look like when equilibrium is reached?

   _____

   _____

   _____

30. **Predicting** Once equilibrium is reached in the apparatus shown in Figure 2, will the molecules continue to move? Explain your answer.

   _____

   _____

   _____

Essay

Write the answer to each question in the space provided.

31. Summarize three statements from the cell theory. Explain the significance of the cell theory to biology.

32. Compare the cell membrane to a mosaic.

33. How do facilitated diffusion and active transport differ?

34. Compare a cell from a unicellular organism with a cell from a multicellular organism in terms of cell specialization.

35. Discuss the levels of organization in multicellular organisms.

Chapter 7 Cell Structure and Function   **Chapter Test B**

Multiple Choice

Write the letter that best answers the question or completes the statement on the line provided.

_____ 1. Who was the first person to identify and see cells?
   a. Anton van Leeuwenhoek
   b. Robert Hooke
   c. Matthias Schleiden

_____ 2. The thin, flexible barrier around a cell is called the
   a. cell membrane.
   b. cell wall.
   c. cell envelope.

_____ 3. Prokaryotes lack
   a. cytoplasm.
   b. a cell membrane.
   c. a nucleus.

_____ 4. Which of the following contains a nucleus?
   a. prokaryotes
   b. bacteria
   c. eukaryotes

_____ 5. The main function of the cell wall is to
   a. support and protect the cell.
   b. store DNA.
   c. direct the activities of the cell.

_____ 6. Which of the following is a function of the nucleus?
   a. controls most of the cell's processes
   b. contains the information needed to make proteins
   c. both a and b

_____ 7. Which of the following is a function of the cytoskeleton?
   a. helps a cell keep its shape
   b. contains DNA
   c. surrounds the cell

_____ **8.** Which of the following is an organelle found in the cytoplasm?

    a. nucleolus

    b. ribosome

    c. chromatin

_____ **9.** Which organelle would you expect to find in plant cells?

    a. mitochondrion

    b. ribosome

    c. chloroplast

_____ **10.** Which of the following structures serves as the cell's boundary from its environment?

    a. mitochondrion

    b. cell membrane

    c. chloroplast

_____ **11.** Diffusion is the movement of particles from

    a. an area of low concentration to an area of high concentration.

    b. an area of high concentration to an area of low concentration.

    c. an area of equilibrium to an area of high concentration.

_____ **12.** The diffusion of water across a selectively permeable membrane is called

    a. osmotic pressure.

    b. osmosis.

    c. facilitated diffusion.

_____ **13.** Which term refers to cells having different tasks in an organism?

    a. multicellular

    b. cell specialization

    c. levels of organization

_____ **14.** Which of the following is an example of an organ?

    a. heart

    b. epithelial tissue

    c. digestive system

_____ **15.** A group of similar cells that perform a particular function is called a(an)

    a. organ.

    b. organ system.

    c. tissue.

Completion

Complete each statement on the line provided.

16. The portion of the cell outside the nucleus is called the _____ .

17. Eukaryotes contain structures that act as if they are specialized organs. These structures are called _____ .

18. Molecules tend to move from an area where they are more concentrated to an area where they are less concentrated. This process is called _____ .

19. The cells in a multicellular organism have specific jobs. This is called cell _____ .

20. The levels of organization in a multicellular organism are _____ , tissues, _____ , and organ systems.

Short Answer

In complete sentences, write the answers to the questions on the lines provided.

21. What does the cell theory state?

_____

_____

_____

22. What are two functions of the nucleus?

_____

_____

23. List two functions of the cytoskeleton.

_____

_____

_____

24. Explain, in terms of osmosis, why a raisin placed in a cup of pure water overnight will puff up with water.

_____

_____

_____

25. List the four levels of organization in order from simplest to most complex.

_____

_____

Using Science Skills

Use the diagrams below to answer the following questions on the lines provided.

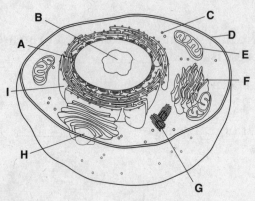

Figure 1

Diagram I

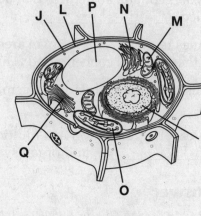

Diagram II

26. **Interpreting Graphics** Which diagram in Figure 1 contains a structure that captures sunlight and converts it into chemical energy? What is the name of the structure described?

_____

_____

27. **Comparing and Contrasting** Look at Figure 1. Give the letter of the structure in diagram I of Figure 1 that corresponds to structure L in diagram II. What is the name of this structure?

_____

_____

28. **Interpreting Graphics** What is the cell membrane labelled in diagram I? In diagram II?

_____

29. **Interpreting Graphics** Which organelle is labeled P in Figure 1? What is the function of this organelle?

_____

_____

30. **Interpreting Graphics** Do the drawings in Figure 1 represent prokaryotes or eukaryotes? How do you know?

_____

_____

LESSON PLAN 8–1 (pages 201–203)

Energy and Life

Section Objectives

Local Standards

- **8.1.1 Explain** where plants get the energy they need to produce food.
- **8.1.2 Describe** the role of ATP in cellular activities.

Vocabulary autotroph • heterotroph
• adenosine triphosphate (ATP)

1 FOCUS

Reading Strategy
Have students write a question for each section head and subhead.

Targeted Resources
❑ Transparencies: **110** Section 8–1 Interest Grabber
❑ Transparencies: **111** Section 8–1 Outline

2 INSTRUCT

Build Science Skills: Classifying
Students classify living things as autotrophs or heterotrophs. **L2**

Address Misconceptions
Review the concept that natural processes occur automatically. **L1 L2**

Use Visuals: Figure 8–2
Use Figure 8–2 to review ATP composition and how removing the third phosphate group releases energy. **L2**

Make Connections: Chemistry
Use a large spring to clarify how stored energy is released from ATP. **L2**

Build Science Skills: Using Analogies
Draw an analogy between the storage molecules ATP and glucose with that of coins and paper money. **L1**

Targeted Resources
❑ Reading and Study Workbook: Section 8–1
❑ Adapted Reading and Study Workbook: Section 8–1
❑ Teaching Resources: Section Summaries 8–1, Worksheets 8–1
❑ Transparencies: **112** ATP, **113** Figure 8–3 Comparison of ADP and ATP to a Battery
❑ **PHSchool.com** ATP

3 ASSESS

Evaluate Understanding
Call on students to explain the differences between autotrophs and heterotrophs and between ATP and ADP.

Reteach
Students make illustrations of ATP and ADP showing how energy is stored and released.

Targeted Resources
❑ Teaching Resources: Section Review 8–1
❑ 〈*i*Text〉 Section 8–1

LESSON PLAN 8–2 (pages 204–207)

Photosynthesis: An Overview

Section Objectives

- **8.2.1 Explain** what the experiments of van Helmont, Priestley, and Ingenhousz reveal about how plants grow.
- **8.2.2 State** the overall equation for photosynthesis.
- **8.2.3 Describe** the role of light and chlorophyll in photosynthesis.

Vocabulary photosynthesis • pigment • chlorophyll

Local Standards

---

1 FOCUS

Reading Strategy
Students use key words under each blue head to write summaries.

Targeted Resources
❏ Transparencies: **114** Section 8–2 Interest Grabber
❏ Transparencies: **115** Section 8–2 Outline

---

2 INSTRUCT

Build Science Skills: Applying Concepts
Draw a large tree with leaves and roots on the board, and ask students what it is that trees obtain from the ground and air. **L1** **L2**

Build Science Skills: Designing Experiments
Students design an experiment similar to Priestley's 1771 experiment. **L2**

Quick Lab
Students observe gas forming on elodea leaves and conclude that oxygen is produced by plants during photosynthesis. **L2** **L3**

Build Science Skills: Using Tables and Graphs
Use the graph in Figure 8–5 to review light absorption by chlorophyll *a* and chlorophyll *b*.
L2

Targeted Resources
❏ Reading and Study Workbook: Section 8–2
❏ Adapted Reading and Study Workbook: Section 8–2
❏ Transparencies: **116** Photosynthesis: Reactants and Products, **117** Figure 8–5 Absorption of Light by Chlorophylls *a* and *b*
❏ Teaching Resources: Section Summaries 8–1, Worksheets 8–1, Enrichment
❏ Lab Manual A: Chapter 8 Lab
❏ Lab Manual B: Chapter 8 Lab

---

3 ASSESS

Evaluate Understanding
Students explain how plants produce sugars through photosynthesis.

Reteach
Students make labeled drawings of realistic objects showing the process of photosynthesis, based on the diagram in Figure 8–4.

Targeted Resources
❏ Teaching Resources: Section Review 8–2
❏ ⟨i**Text**⟩ Section 8–2

LESSON PLAN 8–3 (pages 208–214)

The Reactions of Photosynthesis

Time
2 periods
1 block

Section Objectives
Local Standards

- **8.3.1 Describe** the structure and function of a chloroplast.
- **8.3.2 Describe** what happens in the light-dependent reactions.
- **8.3.3 Explain** what the Calvin cycle is.
- **8.3.4 Identify** factors that affect the rate at which photosynthesis occurs.

Vocabulary thylakoid • photosystem • stroma • $NADP^+$ • light-dependent reactions • ATP synthase • Calvin cycle

1 FOCUS

Vocabulary Preview
Have students find the Vocabulary words within the section and preview their meanings.

Targeted Resources
❑ Transparencies: **118** Section 8–3 Interest Grabber
❑ Transparencies: **119** Section 8–3 Outline
❑ Transparencies: **120** Concept Map

2 INSTRUCT

Use Visuals: Figure 8–7
Use Figure 8–7 to review an overview of the process of photosynthesis. **L1 L2**

Make Connections: Physics
Review basic concepts related to light, including wavelengths and photons. **L1 L2**

Demonstration
Reinforce the concept that light-dependent reactions require light by using two plants. Place one plant in a sunny location and one in a dark place. Water both plants every other day. At the end of one week, the plant that received sunlight should look healthy, while the other plant will look unhealthy. **L1 L2**

Use Visuals: Figure 8–11
Use Figure 8–11 to review events of the Calvin cycle. **L2**

Analyzing Data
Students analyze a graph to determine how levels of light affect photosynthesis. **L2**

Targeted Resources
❑ Reading and Study Workbook: Section 8–3
❑ Adapted Reading and Study Workbook: Section 8–3
❑ Teaching Resources: Section Summaries 8–3, Worksheets 8–3
❑ Transparencies: **121** Figure 8–7 Photosynthesis: An Overview, **122** Figure 8–10 Light-Dependent Reactions, **123** Figure 8–11 Calvin Cycle
❑ Lab Worksheets: Chapter 8 Design an Experiment
❑ **NSTA** *sciLINKS* Calvin Cycle
❑ **NSTA** *sciLINKS* Photosynthesis

3 ASSESS

Evaluate Understanding
Call on students to define or explain each of the section's Vocabulary words.

Reteach
Students describe parts of Figures 8–10 and 8–11, in the sequence in which events occur.

Targeted Resources
❑ Teaching Resources: Section Review 8–3, Chapter Vocabulary Review, Graphic Organizer, Chapter 8 Tests: Levels A and B
❑ **iText** Section 8–3, Chapter 8 Assessment
❑ **PHSchool.com** Online Chapter 8 Test

Chapter 8   Photosynthesis

Summary

8-1 Energy and Life

Plants and some other living things can use light energy from the sun to make food. These organisms are called **autotrophs.** Many organisms cannot use the sun's energy directly. These organisms, called **heterotrophs**, get energy from their food.

Adenosine triphosphate, or ATP, is a compound cells use to store and release energy. **ATP is the basic energy source of all cells.** Cells use energy from ATP to carry out many activities. These include active transport, synthesis of proteins and nucleic acids, and responses to chemical signals at the cell surface. ATP is made up of adenine, a 5-carbon sugar called ribose, and three phosphate groups.

Adenosine diphosphate (ADP) is a compound similar to ATP. Unlike ATP, ADP has only two phosphate groups. When energy is available, a cell can store small amounts of energy by adding a phosphate group to ADP to form ATP (ADP + P → ATP). Energy stored in ATP is released by breaking the bond between the second and third phosphate groups (ATP → ADP + P).

8-2 Photosynthesis: An Overview

Research into photosynthesis began centuries ago. **The experiments of van Helmont, Priestly, and Ingenhousz led to work by other scientists. These scientists found that in the presence of light, plants change carbon dioxide and water into carbohydrates and give off oxygen.** This process is called **photosynthesis.**

The overall equation for photosynthesis is:

$$6CO_2 + 6H_2O \xrightarrow{\text{light}} C_6H_{12}O_6 + 6O_2$$

$$\text{carbon dioxide} + \text{water light} \xrightarrow{\text{light}} \text{sugars} + \text{oxygen}$$

Photosynthesis uses the energy of sunlight to convert water and carbon dioxide into high-energy sugars and oxygen. Plants get the carbon dioxide needed for photosynthesis from the air or from the water in which they grow. Plants use the sugars produced during photosynthesis to make complex carbohydrates such as starches.

Photosynthesis also requires light and chlorophyll. Plants gather the sun's energy with light-absorbing molecules called **pigments.** The main pigment in plants is **chlorophyll.** A compound that absorbs light also absorbs the light's energy. When chlorophyll absorbs sunlight, much of the light energy is sent directly to electrons in the chlorophyll molecules. This raises the energy levels of the electrons.

The visible spectrum is made up of wavelengths of light you can see. This spectrum contains all the colors. Chlorophyll absorbs light in the blue-violet and red regions of the visible spectrum well. Chlorophyll does not absorb light in the green region well. Plants look green because their leaves reflect this green light.

8–3 The Reactions of Photosynthesis

In plants and other photosynthetic prokaryotes, photosynthesis takes place inside the chloroplasts. Chloroplasts have saclike photosynthetic membranes called **thylakoids.** Proteins in the thylakoid membrane organize chlorophyll and other pigments into clusters known as **photosystems.** The photosystems are the light-collecting units of chlorophyll.

When sunlight excites electrons in chlorophyll, the electrons gain energy. The electron transfers its energy to another molecule. The energy continues to move from molecule to molecule until it gets to the end of the chain.

The reactions of photosynthesis occur in two parts: light-dependent reactions and light-independent reactions.

1. **The light-dependent reactions produce oxygen gas and convert ADP and NADP$^+$ into ATP and NADPH.** These reactions need light and they occur in the thylakoid membranes. The light-dependent reactions can be divided into four processes: light absorption, oxygen production, electron transport, and ATP formation. The light-dependent reactions use water, ADP, and NADP$^+$. They produce oxygen, ATP, and NADPH.

2. The light-independent reactions are also called the Calvin cycle. These reactions do not need light. **The Calvin cycle uses ATP and NADPH from the light-dependent reactions to produce high-energy sugars.** The Calvin cycle takes place in the **stroma** of chloroplasts. The Calvin cycle uses carbon dioxide in its reactions. As photosynthesis proceeds, the Calvin cycle works steadily to remove carbon dioxide from the atmosphere and turn out energy-rich sugars. Six carbon dioxide molecules are needed to make a single 6-carbon sugar.

Many factors affect the rate of photosynthesis. Such factors include water availability, temperature, and the intensity of light.

ATP

ATP is the basic energy source of all cells. Energy is stored by cells when ADP is converted into ATP. Energy is released when ATP loses a phosphate and becomes ADP.

Label the energy storing *reaction and the* energy releasing *reaction.*

ADP   +   Phosphate ⟶   ATP

_____

ATP   ⟶   ADP   +   Phosphate

_____

Answer the questions.

1. How many phosphate groups are in one molecule of ATP?

_____

2. How many phosphate groups are in one molecule of ADP?

_____

3. What are the three parts of an ATP molecule?

_____

The Chloroplast

In plants, photosynthesis takes place in chloroplasts. Inside chloroplasts are saclike membranes called thylakoids. These thylakoids are arranged in stacks. A stack of thylakoids is called a granum. The region outside of the thylakoids, but inside the chloroplast is called the stroma.

In the diagram of the chloroplast, label a thylakoid, *the* stroma, *and the* granum.

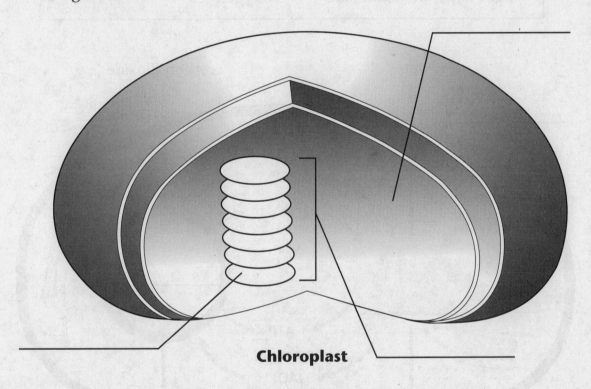

Chloroplast

Answer the following questions. Circle the correct answer.

1. Where are the photosystems, or light-collecting units of photosynthesis, found?

   thylakoid membranes   stroma

2. In what part of the chloroplast does the Calvin cycle take place?

   thylakoid membranes   stroma

3. In what part of the chloroplast do the light-dependent reactions of photosynthesis take place?

   thylakoid membranes   stroma

Photosynthesis Overview

Photosynthesis uses light energy to convert water and carbon dioxide into oxygen and high-energy sugars. The picture below shows an overall view of the process of photosynthesis.

Use the words below to label the diagram.

Calvin cycle	light energy	sugars
light-dependent reactions	oxygen	

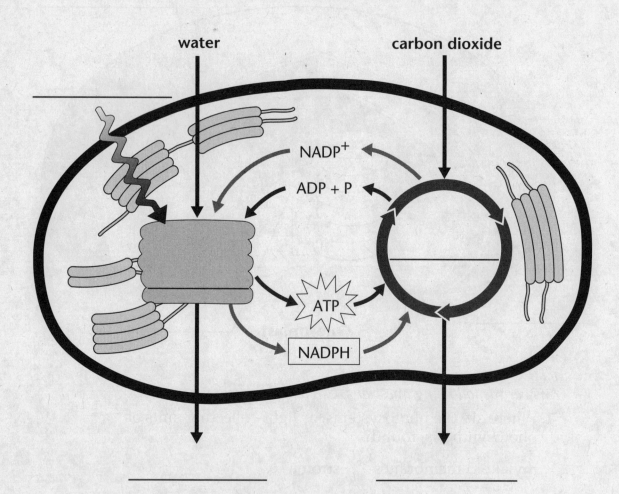

Use the diagram to answer the questions.

1. Finish the equation for photosynthesis.

carbon dioxide + water $\xrightarrow{\text{light}}$ _____

2. Which of the following is also called the light-independent reactions of photosynthesis? Circle the correct answer.

Calvin cycle   electron transport chain

Photosystems I and II

Photosystems I and II are important parts of the light-dependent reactions of photosynthesis. In photosystem II, light energy is absorbed by electrons. These high-energy electrons are then passed down an electron transport chain. The electrons are then passed to photosystem I. In photosytem I, the electrons are reenergized by light energy and used to make NADPH.

Color the diagram according to the prompts below.
- Color the two places where light energy enters the reactions yellow.
- Color the hydrogen ions red.
- Color the electrons green.
- Color the thylakoid membrane blue.

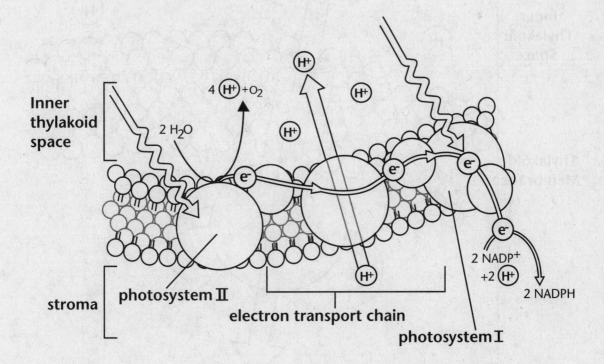

Use the diagram to answer the questions.

1. Where does light energy enter the system?

_____

2. What uses energy from the high-energy electrons to transport hydrogen across the thylakoid membrane? Circle the correct answer.

photosystem II   electron transport chain

ATP Formation in the Light-Dependent Reactions of Photosynthesis

In the light-dependent reactions of photosynthesis, the electron transport chain transports hydrogen ions across the thylakoid membrane. ATP synthase uses these hydrogen ions to power the formation of ATP. Hydrogen ions move through ATP synthase and cause it to spin. As it spins, it forms ATP from ADP and a phosphate.

Color the arrow that shows how ATP synthase spins. Then, draw in the formation of ATP from ADP.

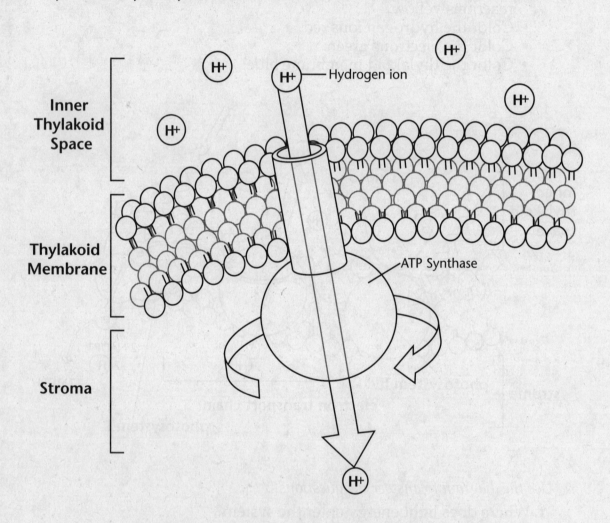

Use the diagram to answer the question. Circle the correct answer.

1. Where does the formation of ATP take place?

inner thylakoid space   stroma

The Calvin Cycle

ATP and NADPH are both produced by the light-dependent reactions of photosynthesis. The Calvin cycle uses the energy in ATP and NADPH to produce high-energy sugars.

Circle the places where ATP and NADPH are used. Then, draw an X over the 6-carbon high-energy sugar produced by the Calvin cycle.

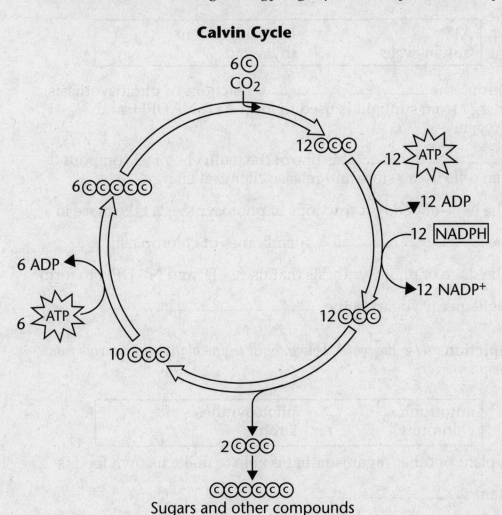

Calvin Cycle

Sugars and other compounds

Use the diagram to answer the question.

1. How many molecules of carbon dioxide are used to produce one 6-carbon sugar molecule?

_____

2. What is formed as a result of the Calvin cycle? Circle the correct answer.

   six-carbon sugar   carbon dioxide

Chapter 8   Photosynthesis

Vocabulary Review

Completion   *Use the words below to fill in the blanks with terms from the chapter.*

ATP	light-dependent
Calvin cycle	thylakoid

1. During the _____ reactions of photosynthesis, energy from sunlight is used to form ATP, NADPH, and oxygen.

2. _____ is one of the main chemical compounds that cells use to store and release chemical energy.

3. The light-dependent reactions of photosynthesis take place in the _____ membranes of chloroplasts.

4. The stage of photosynthesis that uses ATP and NADPH to form high-energy sugars is the _____.

Completion   *Use the words below to fill in the blanks with terms from the chapter.*

autotroph	photosynthesis
chlorophyll	stroma

5. A plant or other organism that is able to make its own food is a(an) _____.

6. _____ is the overall process in which sunlight is used to convert carbon dioxide and water into oxygen and high-energy sugars.

7. The region of the chloroplast in which the Calvin cycle occurs is the _____.

8. The principle pigment in plants is called

_____.

Summary

8–1 Energy and Life

Plants and some other types of organisms are able to use light energy from the sun to produce food. Organisms that make their own food are called autotrophs. Other organisms cannot use the sun's energy directly. These organisms, called heterotrophs, obtain energy from the foods they consume.

One of the principal chemical compounds that cells use to store and release energy is adenosine triphosphate, or ATP. ATP consists of adenine, a 5-carbon sugar called ribose, and three phosphate groups. Adenosine diphosphate (ADP) is a similar compound that has only two phosphate groups instead of three. When a cell has energy available, it can store small amounts of energy by adding a third phosphate group to ADP, producing ATP. The energy stored in ATP can be released by breaking the bond between the second and third phosphate groups. Because a cell can subtract this third phosphate group, it can release energy as needed. The characteristics of ATP make it exceptionally useful as the basic energy source of all cells. Cells use energy from ATP to carry out many important activities, including active transport, synthesis of proteins and nucleic acids, and responses to chemical signals at the cell surface. Cells store a small amount of ATP because ATP is easy to regenerate from ADP. When ATP is needed, cells use the energy in foods such as glucose to produce ATP.

8–2 Photosynthesis: An Overview

Research into photosynthesis began centuries ago. In 1643, Jan van Helmont concluded that trees gain most of their mass from water. In 1771, Joseph Priestley determined that plants release oxygen, which can keep a candle burning.

In 1779, Jan Ingenhousz concluded that plants need sunlight to produce oxygen. The experiments performed by van Helmont, Priestley, and Ingenhousz led to work by other scientists who finally discovered that in the presence of light, plants transform carbon dioxide and water into carbohydrates and plants also release oxygen.

The overall equation for photosynthesis can be shown as follows:

$$6CO_2 + 6\ H_2O \xrightarrow{\text{light}} C_6H_{12}O_6 + 6O_2$$

$$\text{carbon dioxide} + \text{water} \xrightarrow{\text{light}} \text{sugars} + \text{oxygen}$$

Photosynthesis uses the energy of sunlight to convert water and carbon dioxide into high-energy sugars and oxygen. Plants use the sugars to produce complex carbohydrates such as starches. Plants obtain the carbon dioxide they need for photosynthesis from the air or from the water in which they grow.

In addition to water and carbon dioxide, photosynthesis requires light and chlorophyll. Plants gather the sun's energy with light-absorbing molecules called pigments. The plants' principal pigment is chlorophyll. There are two main types of chlorophyll: chlorophyll *a* and chlorophyll *b*.

The wavelengths of sunlight you can see make up the visible spectrum, which contains all the colors. Chlorophyll absorbs light in the blue-violet and red regions very well. But it does not absorb light in the green region well. Green light is reflected by leaves, which is why plants look green.

Any compound that absorbs light absorbs the energy in light. When chlorophyll absorbs sunlight, much of the energy of the light is transferred directly to the electrons in the chlorophyll molecule, raising the energy level of the electrons.

8–3 The Reactions of Photosynthesis

In plants and other photosynthetic prokaryotes, photosynthesis takes place inside the chloroplasts. Chloroplasts contain saclike photosynthetic membranes called thylakoids. Thylakoids are arranged in stacks called grana. Proteins in the thylakoid membrane organize chlorophyll and other pigments into clusters known as photosystems. These photosystems are the light-collecting units of chlorophyll. The reactions of photosynthesis occur in two parts: (1) the light-dependent reactions and (2) the light-independent reactions, also known as the Calvin cycle. The light-dependent reactions take place within the thylakoid membranes. The Calvin cycle takes place in the stroma—the region outside of the thylakoid membranes.

When sunlight excites electrons in chlorophyll, the electrons gain a great deal of energy. A carrier molecule is a compound that can accept a pair of high-energy electrons and transfer them along with most of their energy to another molecule. One of these carrier molecules is $NADP^+$. In the process of photosynthesis, $NADP^+$ accepts and holds 2 high-energy electrons along with a hydrogen ion (H^+). This converts the $NADP^+$ into NADPH.

The light-dependent reactions require light. These reactions use energy from light to produce oxygen gas and convert ADP and $NADP^+$ into the energy carriers ATP and NADPH. Photosynthesis begins when pigments in photosystem II absorb light. A series of reactions follows. The reactants are water, ADP, and $NADP^+$. The products are oxygen gas, ATP, and NADPH. The oxygen gas produced by photosynthesis is the source of nearly all the oxygen in Earth's atmosphere.

The Calvin cycle does not require light. During the Calvin cycle, plants use the energy of ATP and NADPH—products of the light-dependent reactions—to produce high-energy sugars. The Calvin cycle uses carbon dioxide in its series of reactions. As photosynthesis proceeds, the Calvin cycle works steadily, removing carbon dioxide from the atmosphere and turning out energy-rich sugars. Six carbon dioxide molecules are needed to produce a single 6-carbon sugar.

Many factors affect the rate of photosynthesis. Such factors include availability of water, temperature, and intensity of light.

Chapter 8   Photosynthesis

Section 8–1 Energy and Life (pages 201–203)

Key Concepts
- Where do plants get the energy they need to produce food?
- What is the role of ATP in cellular activities?

Autotrophs and Heterotrophs (page 201)

1. Where does the energy of food originally come from? _____
_____

2. Complete the table describing the types of organisms.

TYPES OF ORGANISMS

Type	Description	Examples
	Organisms that make their own food	
	Organisms that obtain energy from the food they eat	

Chemical Energy and ATP (page 202)

3. What is one of the principal chemical compounds that cells use to store energy?
_____

4. How is ATP different from ADP? _____
_____

5. Label each part of the ATP molecule illustrated below.

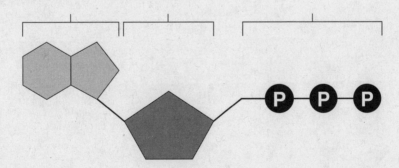

6. When a cell has energy available, how can it store small amounts of that energy?
_____
_____

7. When is the energy stored in ATP released? _____
_____
_____

8. For what purpose do the characteristics of ATP make it exceptionally useful to all types of cells? _____
_____

9. What are two ways in which cells use the energy provided by ATP?

a. _____

b. _____

Using Biochemical Energy (pages 202–203)

10. Why is it efficient for cells to keep only a small supply of ATP on hand?
_____
_____
_____

11. Circle the letter of where cells get the energy to regenerate ATP.

a. ADP

b. phosphates

c. foods like glucose

d. organelles

Section 8–2 Photosynthesis:
An Overview (pages 204–207)

⊂▭⊃ Key Concepts
- What did the experiments of van Helmont, Priestley, and Ingenhousz reveal about how plants grow?
- What is the overall equation for photosynthesis?
- What is the role of light and chlorophyll in photosynthesis?

Introduction (page 204)

1. What occurs in the process of photosynthesis? _____

_____

_____

Investigating Photosynthesis (pages 204–206)

2. What did Jan van Helmont conclude from his experiment? _____

_____

_____

3. Circle the letter of the substance produced by the mint plant in Joseph Priestley's experiment.

   a. carbon dioxide

   b. water

   c. air

   d. oxygen

4. What did Jan Ingenhousz show? _____

_____

_____

The Photosynthesis Equation (page 206)

5. Write the overall equation for photosynthesis using words.

_____

6. Photosynthesis uses the energy of sunlight to convert water and

   carbon dioxide into oxygen and high-energy _____.

Light and Pigments (page 207)

7. What does photosynthesis require in addition to water and carbon dioxide?

_____

_____

8. Plants gather the sun's energy with light-absorbing molecules called _____.

9. What is the principal pigment of plants? _____

10. Circle the letters of the regions of the visible spectrum in which chlorophyll absorbs light very well.

    a. blue-violet region

    b. green region

    c. red region

    d. yellow region

Reading Skill Practice

By looking at illustrations in textbooks, you can help yourself remember better what you have read. Look carefully at Figure 8–4 on page 206. What important ideas does this illustration communicate? Do your work on a separate sheet of paper.

Section 8–3 The Reactions of Photosynthesis
(pages 208–214)

👁 Key Concepts
- What happens in the light-dependent reactions?
- What is the Calvin cycle?

Inside a Chloroplast (page 208)

1. Chloroplasts contain saclike photosynthetic membranes called _____.

2. What is a granum? _____

_____

3. The region outside the thylakoid membranes in the chloroplasts is called the

_____.

4. What are the two stages of photosynthesis called?

a. _____

b. _____

5. Complete the illustration of the overview of photosynthesis by writing the products
   and the reactants of the process, as well as the energy source that excites the electrons.

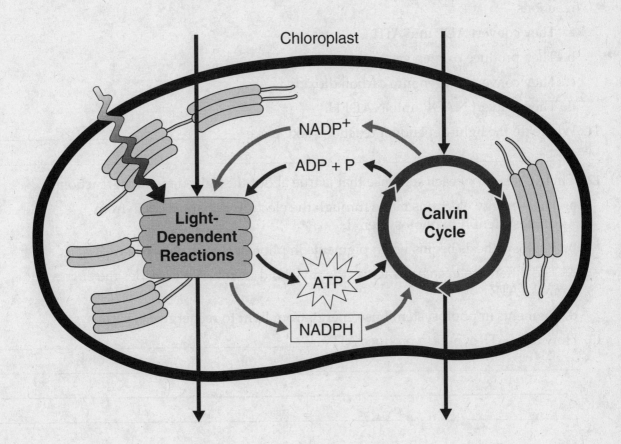

Electron Carriers (page 209)

6. When sunlight excites electrons in chlorophyll, how do the electrons change?

_____

_____

7. What is a carrier molecule? _____

_____

_____

_____

8. Circle the letter of the carrier molecule involved in photosynthesis.

    a. H_2O **c.** CO_2

    b. $NADP^+$ **d.** O_2

9. How does $NADP^+$ become NADPH? _____

_____

_____

Light-Dependent Reactions (pages 210–211)

10. Circle the letter of each sentence that is true about the light-dependent reactions.

    a. They convert ADP into ATP.

    b. They produce oxygen gas.

    c. They convert oxygen into carbon dioxide.

    d. They convert $NADP^+$ into NADPH.

11. Where do the light-dependent reactions take place? _____

_____

12. Circle the letter of each sentence that is true about the light-dependent reactions.

    a. High-energy electrons move through the electron transport chain from photosystem II to photosystem I.

    b. Photosynthesis begins when pigments in photosystem I absorb light.

    c. The difference in charges across the thylakoid membrane provides the energy to make ATP.

    d. Pigments in photosystem I use energy from light to reenergize electrons.

13. How does ATP synthase produce ATP? _____

_____

_____

_____

The Calvin Cycle (pages 212–214)

14. What does the Calvin cycle use to produce high-energy sugars?

_____

_____

15. Why are the reactions of the Calvin cycle also called the light-independent reactions?

_____

16. Circle the letter of each statement that is true about the Calvin cycle.

   a. The main products of the Calvin cycle are six carbon dioxide molecules.

   b. Carbon dioxide molecules enter the Calvin cycle from the atmosphere.

   c. Energy from ATP and high-energy electrons from NADPH are used to convert 3-carbon molecules into higher-energy forms.

   d. The Calvin cycle uses six molecules of carbon dioxide to produce a single 6-carbon sugar molecule.

Factors Affecting Photosynthesis (page 214)

17. What are three factors that affect the rate at which photosynthesis occurs?

   a. _____

   b. _____

   c. _____

18. Is the following sentence true or false? Increasing the intensity of light decreases the rate of photosynthesis. _____

Chapter 8   Photosynthesis

Vocabulary Review

Matching   *In the space provided, write the letter of the definition that best matches each term.*

_____ 1. photosynthesis

_____ 2. chlorophyll

_____ 3. pigment

_____ 4. adenosine triphosphate

_____ 5. thylakoid

_____ 6. photosystems

_____ 7. stroma

_____ 8. NADP⁺

_____ 9. Calvin cycle

_____ 10. light-dependent reactions

a. clusters in the thylakoid membrane of chlorophyll and other pigments

b. the region of the chloroplast outside the thylakoid membranes

c. electron carrier

d. process in which plants use the energy of sunlight to make high-energy carbohydrates

e. reactions that use ATP and NADPH to produce high-energy sugars

f. light-absorbing molecules

g. the basic energy source of all cells

h. reactions that produce oxygen gas and convert ADP and NADP⁺ into the energy carriers ATP and NADPH

i. saclike photosynthetic membranes in chloroplasts

j. principal pigment of plants

Answering Questions   *In the space provided, write an answer to each question.*

11. What is an organism that obtains energy from the food it consumes? _____

_____

12. What is an organism that is able to make its own food? _____

_____

13. What is released when the chemical bond is broken between the second and third

phosphates of an ATP molecule? _____

_____

14. What are the reactants of the equation for photosynthesis? _____

_____

15. What are the products of the equation for photosynthesis? _____

_____

Name_____ Class_____ Date _____

Reviewing Key Concepts

Short Answer *On the lines provided, answer the following questions.*

1. Where do autotrophs get energy to produce food?

   _____

   _____

2. How do living things use ATP?

   _____

   _____

3. How is one molecule of ATP formed from one molecule of ADP?

   _____

   _____

4. How does a change from ATP to ADP provide an organism with energy?

   _____

   _____

5. What are two ways in which cells use the energy provided by ATP?

   _____

   _____

Reviewing Key Skills

6. **Comparing and Contrasting** What are the similarities between autotrophs and heterotrophs? What are the differences?

   _____

   _____

   _____

   _____

Classifying *On the line beneath each picture, classify the organism as either* an autotroph *or a* heterotroph.

7.    8.    9.

_____   _____   _____

Reviewing Key Concepts

Matching *Match each scientist with the appropriate experiment or conclusion. Write the letter of the correct scientist on the line provided. A letter may be used more than once.*

   a. Priestley   b. van Helmont   c. Ingenhousz

_____ **1.** Plants need sunlight to produce oxygen.

_____ **2.** Plants gain most of their mass by taking in water.

_____ **3.** Using a candle and a jar, he observed that plants produce a substance that kept the candle burning.

_____ **4.** He measured the mass of the soil in which a plant grew.

_____ **5.** He observed plants exposed to light.

Short Answer *On the lines provided, answer the following questions.*

6. What is the overall equation for photosynthesis?

_____

_____

7. Explain how light energy affects a chlorophyll molecule.

_____

_____

Reviewing Key Skills

8. Predicting If a plant is kept under green-colored light for an extended period of time, what will happen to the plant's food production?

_____

_____

9. Inferring A plant that has a high amount of the orange pigment carotene would have leaves of what color? Explain your answer.

_____

_____

10. Design an Experiment Design an experiment to test the effects of air pollution on plants. Be sure to include a control.

_____

_____

_____

_____

_____

Reviewing Key Concepts

Completion *On the lines provided, complete the following sentences.*

1. The light-dependent reactions take place within the

   _____ membranes.

2. The light-independent reactions are also known as the

   _____.

3. The energy carriers _____ and _____
   are produced during the light-dependent reactions.

4. In the light-dependent reactions, the gas _____ is
   produced.

5. High-energy sugars are produced during the _____
   reactions.

6. The light-independent reactions take place in the

   _____.

Reviewing Key Skills

7. **Comparing and Contrasting** How are photosystem I and
   photosystem II similar? How are they different?

   _____

   _____

   _____

8. **Predicting** If there is no light coming into the chloroplasts, how will
   this affect the Calvin cycle?

   _____

   _____

   _____

9. **Applying Concepts** What effect does weather have on the process
   of photosynthesis?

   _____

   _____

   _____

10. **Applying Concepts** If you place a plant in a clear, sealed box, how
    could you use a measurement of the gases in the boxed air to
    measure the rate of photosynthesis? What gas would you measure?

    _____

    _____

    _____

Chapter 8 Photosynthesis   **Chapter Vocabulary Review**

Defining Terms *On the lines provided, write a definition of each of the following terms.*

1. ATP _____
   _____
   _____

2. thylakoid _____
   _____
   _____

3. NADP⁺ _____

3. $NADP^+$ _____
   _____
   _____

4. ATP synthase _____
   _____
   _____

5. Calvin cycle _____
   _____
   _____

Short Answer *On the lines provided, answer the following questions.*

6. What is the difference between an autotroph and a heterotroph?
   _____
   _____

7. In which part of photosynthesis is oxygen produced?
   _____
   _____

8. What is the relationship between pigments and chlorophyll?
   _____
   _____

9. How do the light-dependent reactions differ from the Calvin cycle?
   _____
   _____

10. What compounds are formed from carbon dioxide in the Calvin cycle?
    _____
    _____

Name_____ Class_____ Date _____

Matching *Match each term with its description below. Write the letter of the correct term on the line provided.*

a. chlorophyll
b. stroma
c. pigment
d. photosynthesis
e. light-dependent reactions

_____ 11. molecule that absorbs light

_____ 12. produce oxygen gas and convert ADP to ATP

_____ 13. the region outside the thylakoid membranes

_____ 14. principal pigment found in plants

_____ 15. process by which autotrophs use sunlight to make high-energy sugars

Labeling Diagrams *On the lines provided, write the names of the reactants and products for photosynthesis that correspond to the numbers in the diagram.*

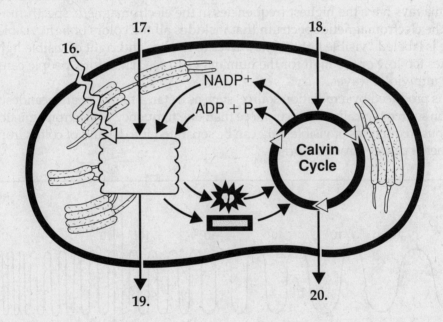

16. _____
17. _____
18. _____
19. _____
20. _____

Chapter 8 Photosynthesis — Enrichment

The Electromagnetic Spectrum

Light is actually energy that is emitted from atoms. Atoms emit light in tiny packets of energy called photons. Photons move through space as electromagnetic waves, which are a form of energy with magnetic and electrical components. The electromagnetic waves that are visible to the human eye are called lightwaves.

Light is only one kind of electromagnetic wave. You may be familiar with other kinds of electromagnetic waves, such as X-rays, microwaves, and radio waves. They are all radiated by vibrating electrons within atoms. The full range of electromagnetic waves is called the electromagnetic spectrum. The main differences between the types of electromagnetic waves are the frequency and wavelength of the radiation.

An illustration of the electromagnetic spectrum appears below. Notice that it is a continuous range of waves. As you move across the spectrum, the frequency and wavelength of the waves vary. All the waves in the electromagnetic spectrum travel through empty space at the same velocity: 299,792,458 m per second.

In the illustration, radio waves are at the left side of the spectrum. Radio waves include AM, FM, shortwave radio, television, and some kinds of radar. In the middle of the spectrum are microwaves and infrared waves. Microwaves include certain kinds of radar. At the right of the spectrum are visible light, ultraviolet light, X-rays, and gamma rays. Note that gamma rays have the highest frequencies in the electromagnetic spectrum.

The part of the electromagnetic spectrum that includes all the colors of light visible to the human eye is labeled "visible light." The waves to the left and right of visible light have frequencies too low or too high for the human eye to see. Therefore, people cannot see infrared or ultraviolet waves.

Visible light is produced by a radiation source, such as a star, a flame, or an incandescent light. A radiation source typically produces more than one frequency of electromagnetic wave. The various frequencies of visible light can be separated into a band of colors from red to violet when it passes through a prism.

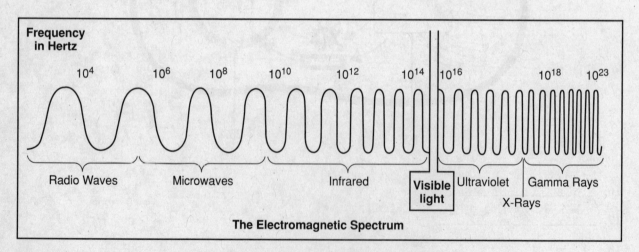

The Electromagnetic Spectrum

Evaluation *Answer the following questions on a separate sheet of paper.*

1. What kind of electromagnetic waves have the longest wavelength? Which ones have the shortest?

2. Bees can see higher frequencies of electromagnetic waves than humans can. What type of electromagnetic radiation do you think bees can see that humans cannot? Explain your answer.

Chapter 8 Photosynthesis   **Graphic Organizer**

Flowchart

The following flowchart represents the reactions of photosynthesis. Fill in the missing information using the formulas listed below.

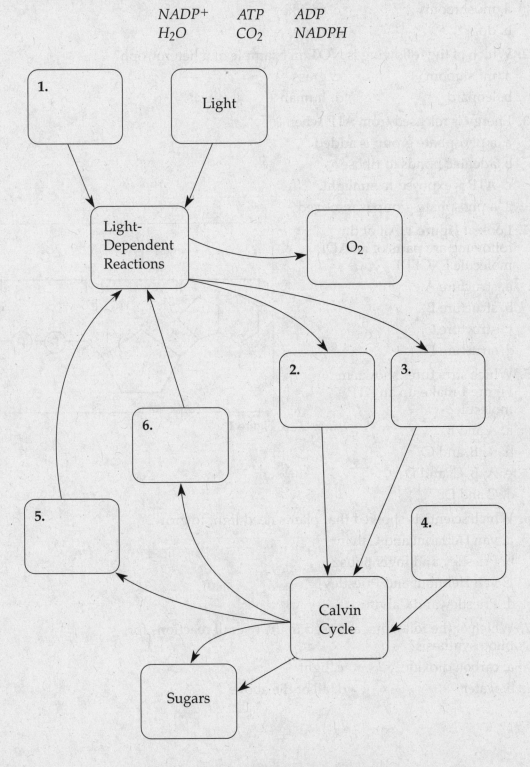

NADP+   ATP   ADP
H_2O CO_2 NADPH

Chapter 8 Photosynthesis   **Chapter Test A**

Multiple Choice

Write the letter that best answers the question or completes the statement on the line provided.

_____ **1.** Which of the following is an autotroph?
    a. mushroom   c. monkey
    b. dog   d. tree

_____ **2.** Which of the following is NOT an example of a heterotroph?
    a. mushroom   c. grass
    b. leopard   d. human

_____ **3.** Energy is released from ATP when
    a. a phosphate group is added.
    b. adenine bonds to ribose.
    c. ATP is exposed to sunlight.
    d. a phosphate group is removed.

_____ **4.** Look at Figure 1. All of the following are parts of an ADP molecule EXCEPT
    a. structure A.
    b. structure B.
    c. structure C.
    d. structure D.

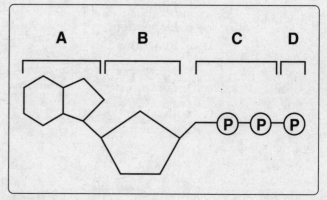

_____ **5.** Which structures shown in Figure 1 make up an ATP molecule?
    a. A and B
    b. A, B, and C
    c. A, B, C, and D
    d. C and D

Figure 1

_____ **6.** Which scientists showed that plants need light to grow?
    a. van Helmont and Calvin
    b. Priestley and Ingenhousz
    c. van Helmont and Priestley
    d. Priestley and Calvin

_____ **7.** Which of the following are used in the overall reactions for photosynthesis?
    a. carbon dioxide   c. light
    b. water   d. all of the above

_____ **8.** Most plants appear green because chlorophyll
   a. does not absorb green light.
   b. reflects violet light.
   c. absorbs green light.
   d. none of the above

_____ **9.** A granum is a(an)
   a. stack of chloroplasts.
   b. stack of thylakoids.
   c. membrane enclosing a thylakoid.
   d. photosynthetic pigment molecule.

_____ **10.** The light-collecting units of a chloroplast are the
   a. electron carriers.   c. stroma.
   b. photosystems.   d. high-energy sugars.

_____ **11.** What are the products of the light-dependent reactions?
   a. oxygen gas   c. NADPH
   b. ATP   d. all of the above

_____ **12.** Which step is the beginning of photosynthesis?
   a. Pigments in photosystem I absorb light.
   b. Pigments in photosystem II absorb light.
   c. High-energy electrons move through the electron transport chain.
   d. ATP synthase allows H^+ ions to pass through the thylakoid membrane.

_____ **13.** The Calvin cycle takes place in the
   a. stroma.   c. thylakoid membranes.
   b. photosystems.   d. chlorophyll molecules.

_____ **14.** If carbon dioxide is removed from a plant's environment, what would you expect to happen to its production of high-energy sugars?
   a. More sugars will be produced.
   b. No sugars will be produced.
   c. The same number of sugars will be produced but without carbon dioxide.
   d. Carbon dioxide does not affect the production of high-energy sugars in plants.

_____ **15.** If you continue to increase the intensity of light that a plant receives, what happens?
   a. The rate of photosynthesis increases with light intensity.
   b. The rate of photosynthesis decreases with light intensity.
   c. The rate of photosynthesis increases and then levels off.
   d. The rate of photosynthesis does not change.

Name_____ Class_____ Date _____

Completion

Complete each statement on the line provided.

16. Photosynthesis requires light, water, carbon dioxide, and _____ .

17. If you separate the pigments found in a typical plant cell's chloroplasts, you will find _____ , orange, and red pigments.

18. Thylakoids are _____ in color because they contain chlorophyll.

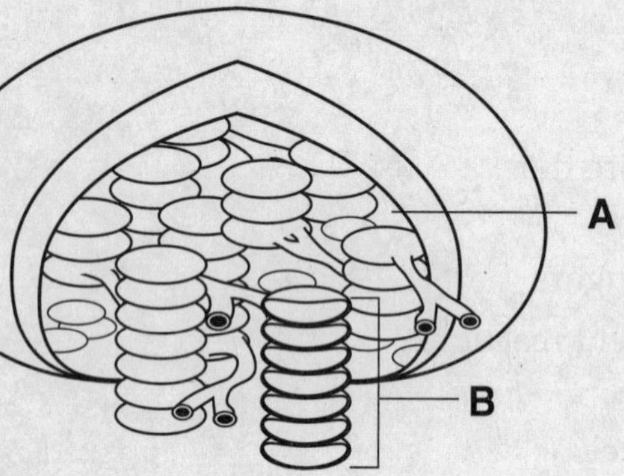

Figure 2

19. Photosystems I and II are found in the structure labeled _____ in Figure 2.

20. In many plants, the rate of photosynthesis _____ when the weather becomes very cold.

Short Answer

In complete sentences, write the answers to the questions on the lines provided.

21. How do heterotrophs obtain energy?

_____

_____

_____

22. What is ATP, and when is energy released from it?

_____

_____

_____

23. Write the overall equation for photosynthesis in both symbols and words.

_____

_____

24. Photosystems I and II are both located in the thylakoid membrane.
What advantage does their proximity provide?

_____

_____

_____

25. What does the Calvin cycle do?

_____

_____

_____

Using Science Skills

*Use the diagram and graph below to answer the following questions on the
lines provided.*

A student prepared two beakers with identical
sprigs of a water plant as shown below. She placed
one beaker in the shade and the other beaker beside a
fluorescent lamp. She then systematically changed the
distance of the beaker from the lamp. She counted the
bubbles given off by each sprig of the water plant.
Shown here is the graph of the data for the beaker she
placed in the light.

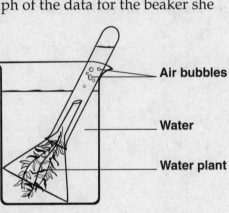

Figure 3

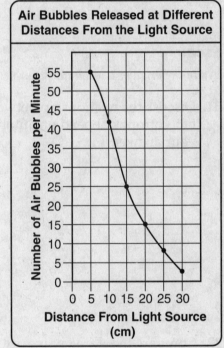

26. Controlling Variables Which beaker is the student's control
beaker, the one in the shade or the one in the light?

_____

27. Applying Concepts Look at Figure 3. If the student later tested the
air bubbles collected in the test tube, what would she find they are
made of? How do you know?

_____

_____

_____

_____

28. **Using Tables and Graphs** Look at the graph in Figure 3. At what distance from the light source was the greatest number of bubbles produced?

_____

29. **Analyzing Data** Look at the graph in Figure 3. What do the student's data show?

_____

_____

30. **Predicting** If the lamp was placed closer than 5 centimeters from the water plant, would the plant give off many more bubbles? Why or why not?

_____

_____

_____

Essay

Write the answer to each question in the space provided.

31. Discuss the relationship between autotrophs and heterotrophs. Do heterotrophs depend on autotrophs for their survival? Explain your answer.

32. Compare the storage capacity of ATP and glucose. How does the cell use each of these molecules to store energy?

33. Describe how pigments obtain energy from light. Use chlorophyll
as an example of the process you describe.

34. Identify three factors that affect the rate of photosynthesis, and
explain the effect of each.

35. Trace the events that occur in the thylakoid membrane during the
light-dependent reactions.

Chapter 8 Photosynthesis   **Chapter Test B**

Multiple Choice

Write the letter that best answers the question or completes the statement on the line provided.

_____ **1.** Organisms that make their own food are called
   a. autotrophs.
   b. heterotrophs.
   c. thylakoids.

_____ **2.** Organisms that cannot make their own food and must obtain energy from the foods they eat are called
   a. autotrophs.
   b. heterotrophs.
   c. thylakoids.

_____ **3.** Which of the following is NOT a part of an ATP molecule?
   a. adenine
   b. ribose
   c. chlorophyll

_____ **4.** In Figure 1, between which parts of the molecule must the bonds be broken to form an ADP molecule?
   a. A and B
   b. B and C
   c. C and D

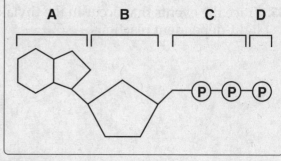

_____ **5.** Jan van Helmont concluded that plants gain most of their mass from
   a. water.
   b. the soil.
   c. carbon dioxide in the air.

Figure 1

_____ **6.** Ingenhousz showed that plants produce oxygen bubbles when exposed to
   a. ATP.
   b. carbon dioxide.
   c. light.

_____ **7.** Photosynthesis uses sunlight to convert water and carbon dioxide into
   a. oxygen.
   b. oxygen and high-energy sugars.
   c. ATP and oxygen.

_____ **8.** Plants gather the sun's energy with light-absorbing molecules called
   a. pigments.
   b. thylakoids.
   c. stroma.

_____ **9.** Plants take in the sun's energy by absorbing

    a. sunlight.

    b. chlorophyll *a*.

    c. chlorophyll *b*.

_____**10.** The stroma is the space that surrounds

    a. thylakoids.

    b. chloroplasts.

    c. plant cells.

_____**11.** Where do the light-dependent reactions take place?

    a. in the stroma

    b. outside the chloroplasts

    c. in the thylakoid membranes

_____**12.** Where are photosystems I and II found?

    a. in the stroma

    b. in the thylakoid membrane

    c. in the Calvin cycle

_____**13.** The Calvin cycle is another name for

    a. light-independent reactions.

    b. light-dependent reactions.

    c. photosynthesis.

_____**14.** What is a product of the Calvin cycle?

    a. oxygen gas

    b. ATP

    c. high-energy sugars

_____**15.** Which of the following affects the rate of photosynthesis?

    a. temperature

    b. light intensity

    c. both a and b

Completion

Complete each statement on the line provided.

16. Organisms, such as hawks and leopards, that obtain energy from the foods they consume are called _____ .

17. Ingenhousz found that plants produce oxygen bubbles only in the presence of

_____ .

18. Photosynthesis uses the energy of sunlight to convert water and carbon dioxide into oxygen and _____ .

Name______________________________ Class____________________ Date ______________

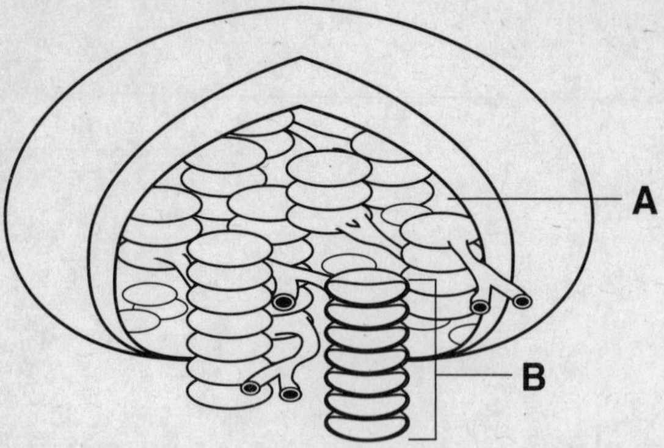

Figure 2

19. The area indicated in Figure 2 by the letter A is called ____________ .

20. The light-dependent reactions convert $NADP^+$ and ADP into the energy carriers NADPH and ____________________ .

Short Answer

In complete sentences, write the answers to the questions on the lines provided.

21. What is the difference between an autotroph and a heterotroph? Give an example of each type of organism.

____

____

____

____

22. Explain how heterotrophs get their energy from the sun even though they cannot make their own food.

____

____

____

____

23. What happens when a phosphate group is removed from an ATP molecule?

____

____

____

24. Identify the structures labeled B in Figure 2. What is their function?

____

____

____

25. List two factors that affect the rate of photosynthesis.

_____

_____

Using Science Skills

Use the diagram below to answer the following questions on the lines provided.

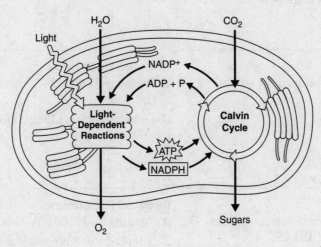

Figure 3

26. Interpreting Graphics What process is shown in Figure 3?

_____

27. Interpreting Graphics What structure is shown in Figure 3?

_____

28. Interpreting Graphics Look at Figure 3. What are the products of the light-dependent reactions?

_____

_____

_____

29. Interpreting Graphics What are the products of the Calvin cycle shown in Figure 3?

_____

30. Interpreting Graphics In Figure 3, what chemical from the atmosphere is used in the Calvin cycle to produce sugars?

_____

LESSON PLAN 9–1 (pages 221–225)

Chemical Pathways

Time
2 periods
1 block

Section Objectives

■ **9.1.1 Explain** what cellular respiration is.

■ **9.1.2 Describe** what happens during the process of glycolysis.

■ **9.1.3 Name** the two main types of fermentation.

Vocabulary calorie • glycolysis • cellular respiration • NAD⁺ • fermentation • anaerobic

Local Standards

---

1 FOCUS

Vocabulary Preview
Call on volunteers to pronounce the section's Vocabulary words.

Targeted Resources
❏ Transparencies: **124** Section 9–1 Interest Grabber

❏ Transparencies: **125** Section 9–1 Outline

---

2 INSTRUCT

Use Visuals: Figure 9–1
Use Figure 9–1 to reinforce the structure and function of mitochondria. **L1 L2**

Use Visuals: Figure 9–2
Use Figure 9–2 to introduce an overview of events in cellular respiration. **L1 L2**

Use Visuals: Figure 9–3
Use Figure 9–3 to review what occurs in the process of glycolysis. **L1**

Build Science Skills: Comparing and Contrasting
Students compare leavened bread and unleavened bread. **L1 L2**

Problem Solving
Students investigate how the production of carbon dioxide can be increased during the making of bread. **L2 L3**

Targeted Resources
❏ Reading and Study Workbook: Section 9–1

❏ Adapted Reading and Study Workbook: Section 9–1

❏ Transparencies: **126** Chemical Pathways, **127** Figure 9–2 Cellular Respiration: An Overview, **128** Figure 9–3 Glycolysis, **129** Figure 9–4 Lactic Acid Fermentation

❏ Teaching Resources: Section Summaries 9–1, Worksheets 9–1, Enrichment

❏ Lab Worksheets: Chapter 9 Real-World Lab

❏ **NSTA** *sci*LINKS Cellular respiration

---

3 ASSESS

Evaluate Understanding
Students explain what occurs during glycolysis and write the equations for alcoholic and lactic acid fermentation.

Reteach
Students make flowcharts that explain the processes of glycolysis, alcoholic fermentation, and lactic acid fermentation.

Targeted Resources
❏ Teaching Resources: Section Review 9–1

❏ *i*Text Section 9–1

LESSON PLAN 9–2 (pages 226–232)

The Krebs Cycle and Electron Transport

Time
3 periods
1 1/2 blocks

Section Objectives

Local Standards

- **9.2.1 Describe** what happens during the Krebs cycle.
- **9.2.2 Explain** how high-energy electrons are used by the electron transport chain.
- **9.2.3 Identify** three pathways the body uses to release energy during exercise.
- **9.2.4 Compare** photosynthesis and cellular respiration.

Vocabulary aerobic • Krebs cycle • electron transport chain

1 FOCUS

Reading Strategy
Have students preview Figure 9–6 and Figure 9–7, write questions, and answer their questions as they read the section.

Targeted Resources
❑ Transparencies: **130** Section 9–2 Interest Grabber
❑ Transparencies: **131** Section 9–2 Outline
❑ Transparencies: **132** Flowchart

2 INSTRUCT

Use Visuals: Figure 9–6
Use Figure 9–6 to review the events of the Krebs cycle. **L2**

Use Visuals: Figure 9–7
Use Figure 9–7 to review the events in the electron transport chain. **L2**

Use Community Resources
Invite an aerobics instructor to discuss aerobic exercise and anaerobic exercise. **L1** **L2**

Quick Lab
Students investigate how exercise affects the disposal of wastes from cellular respiration. **L2**

Build Science Skills: Using Analogies
Use the analogy of going up and down a hill to compare the processes of cellular respiration and photosynthesis. **L2**

Targeted Resources
❑ Reading and Study Workbook: Section 9–2
❑ Adapted Reading and Study Workbook: Section 9–2
❑ Teaching Resources: Section Summaries 9–2, Worksheets 9–2
❑ Transparencies: **133** Figure 9–6 The Krebs Cycle, **134** Figure 9–7 Electron Transport Chain
❑ Lab Manual A: Chapter 9 Lab
❑ Lab Manual B: Chapter 9 Lab
❑ **NSTA** *sciLINKS* Krebs cycle

3 ASSESS

Evaluate Understanding
Call on students to describe the steps of the process of cellular respiration.

Reteach
Students write detailed descriptions of Figure 9–6 and Figure 9–7.

Targeted Resources
❑ Teaching Resources: Section Review 9–2, Chapter Vocabulary Review, Graphic Organizer, Chapter 9 Tests: Levels A and B
❑ **iText** Section 9–2, Chapter 9 Assessment
❑ **PHSchool.com** Online Chapter 9 Test

Chapter 9   Cellular Respiration

Summary

9–1 Chemical Pathways

Food is the energy source for cells. The energy in food is measured in calories. A **calorie** is the amount of energy needed to raise the temperature of 1 gram of water 1 degree Celsius. The Calorie (capital C) used on food labels is equal to 1000 calories.

Cells do not burn glucose or other food compounds. They gradually release the energy. The process begins with a pathway called **glycolysis.**

Glycolysis is the process in which a glucose molecule is split in half. This forms two molecules of pyruvic acid, a 3-carbon compound. Glycolysis takes place in the cytoplasm of a cell. Through glycolysis, the cell gains 2 ATP molecules. In addition, the electron carrier NAD^+ accepts a pair of high-energy electrons, producing NADH. By doing this, NAD^+ helps pass energy from glucose to other pathways in the cell.

When oxygen is not present, fermentation follows glycolysis. **Fermentation** releases energy from food molecules by forming ATP. Fermentation does not need oxygen, so it is said to be **anaerobic.** During fermentation, cells convert NADH back into the electron carrier NAD^+ that is needed for glycolysis. This lets glycolysis continue to make a steady supply of ATP. **The two types of fermentation are alcoholic fermentation and lactic acid fermentation.**

- Yeasts and a few other microorganisms carry out alcoholic fermentation. The equation for alcoholic fermentation after glycolysis is:

  pyruvic acid + NADH → alcohol + CO_2 + NAD^+

- Lactic acid fermentation occurs in muscles during rapid exercise. The equation for lactic acid fermentation after glycolysis is:

  pyruvic acid + NADH → lactic acid + NAD^+

If oxygen is present, the Krebs cycle and electron transport chain follow glycolysis. Together, these pathways make up **cellular respiration. Cellular respiration is the process that releases energy by breaking down glucose and other food molecules in the presence of oxygen.** Cellular respiration takes place in mitochondria. The equation for cellular respiration is:

$6O_2 + C_6H_{12}O_6 \rightarrow 6CO_2 + 6H_2O$ + Energy

oxygen + glucose → carbon dioxide + water + Energy

9–2 The Krebs Cycle and Electron Transport

Cellular respiration requires oxygen, so it is said to be **aerobic.**
The **Krebs cycle** is the second stage of cellular respiration.
**During the Krebs cycle, pyruvic acid is broken down into
carbon dioxide in a series of energy-extracting reactions.**
The Krebs cycle is also known as the citric acid cycle, because
citric acid is one of its first products.

Here are the stages of the Krebs cycle.
- The Krebs cycle starts when pyruvic acid formed by
  glycolysis enters the mitochondrion.
- The pyruvic acid is broken down into carbon dioxide and
  a 2-carbon acetyl group.
- The two carbons of the acetyl group join a 4-carbon compound to produce citric acid. The Krebs cycle continues in
  a series of reactions. In these reactions, two energy carriers
  accept high-energy electrons. NAD^+ is changed to NADH,
  and FAD is changed to $FADH_2$. These molecules carry the
  high-energy electrons to the electron transport chain. The
  carbon dioxide is released as a waste product.

**The electron transport chain uses the high-energy electrons
to change ADP into ATP.** In the electron transport chain, high-
energy electrons move from one carrier protein to the next. At
the end of the chain, oxygen pulls electrons from the final carrier
molecule. These electrons join with hydrogen ions, forming water.

Each transfer along the chain releases a small amount of energy.
ATP synthase uses the energy to produce ATP.

Glycolysis produces 2 ATP molecules from one molecule
of glucose. The Krebs cycle and the electron transport chain let the
cell form 34 ATP molecules per glucose molecule. The total, then,
for cellular respiration is 36 ATP molecules per glucose molecule.

The energy flows in photosynthesis and cellular respiration
occur in opposite directions. On a global level, photosynthesis and
cellular respiration are also opposites. Photosynthesis removes
carbon dioxide from the atmosphere and puts back oxygen.
Cellular respiration removes oxygen from the atmosphere and
puts back carbon dioxide.

The Mitochondrion

In plant and animal cells, the final stages of cellular respiration take place in mitochondria. A mitochondrion has two membranes. The inner membrane is folded up inside the outer membrane. The space between the inner and outer membranes is called the intermembrane space. The space inside the inner membrane is called the matrix.

Label the inner membrane, intermembrane space, matrix, *and* outer membrane.

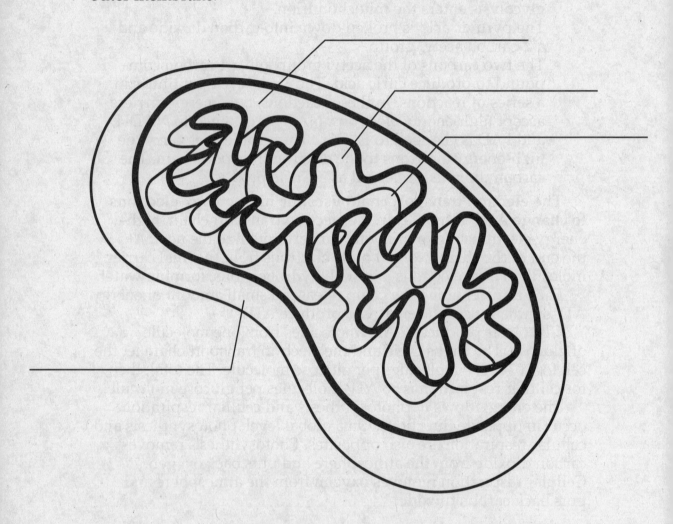

Answer the questions. Circle the correct answer.

1. In which membrane is the electron transport chain located?

outer membrane   inner membrane

Cellular Respiration Overview

Cellular respiration is the process that releases energy from food in the presence of oxygen.

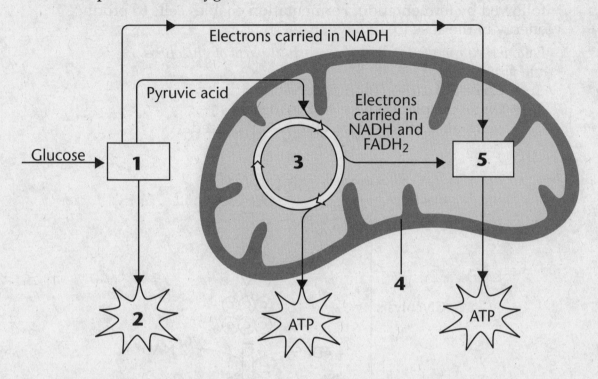

Use the words below to label the diagram of cellular respiration on the lines provided.

ATP	glycolysis	mitochondrion
electron transport chain	Krebs cycle	

1._____

2._____

3._____

4._____

5._____

Use the diagram to answer the questions.

1. Where does glycolysis take place?

_____

2. Where do the Kreb cycle and electron transport chain take place?

_____

Glycolysis and Fermentation

Glycolysis uses ATP to break a molecule of glucose in half, producing pyruvic acid. When oxygen is not present, glycolysis is followed by fermentation. Fermentation enables cells to produce energy in the absence of oxygen.

Follow the prompts to identify important parts of glycolysis and fermentation.

- Color the carbon atoms blue.
- Circle the place where ATP is formed.
- Mark an X on the place where ATP is used.

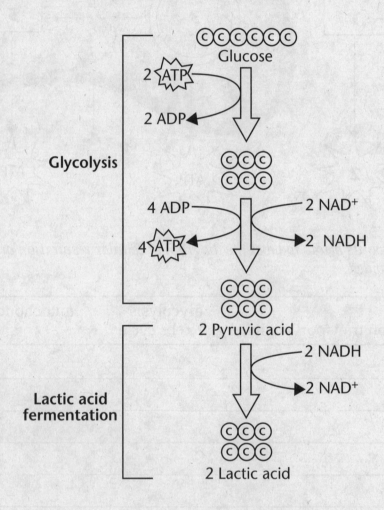

Answer the questions.

1. How many carbon atoms are in one molecule of glucose?

_____

2. What is the product of glycolysis? _____

The Krebs Cycle

If oxygen is present, the pyruvic acid formed during glycolysis moves into the Krebs cycle. The Krebs cycle converts pyruvic acid into carbon dioxide. As carbon dioxide is formed, high energy electrons are accepted by NAD^+ and FAD. This results in the formation of NADH and $FADH_2$. NADH and $FADH_2$ will be used later to produce ATP.

Follow the prompts to identify important parts of the Krebs cycle.
- Color the carbon atoms blue.
- Circle the electron carriers in green.
- Circle ATP in orange.

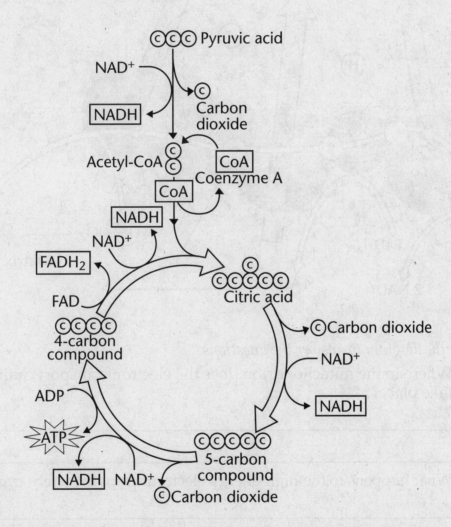

Use the diagram to answer the question. Circle the correct answer.

1. Which of the following is formed during the Krebs cycle?

FADH$_2$ pyruvic acid

Electron Transport Chain

The electron transport chain uses the high-energy electrons produced by the Krebs cycle to move hydrogen ions from one side of the inner membrane to the other.

Label the diagram with the following terms: electron, hydrogen ion, *and* inner membrane.

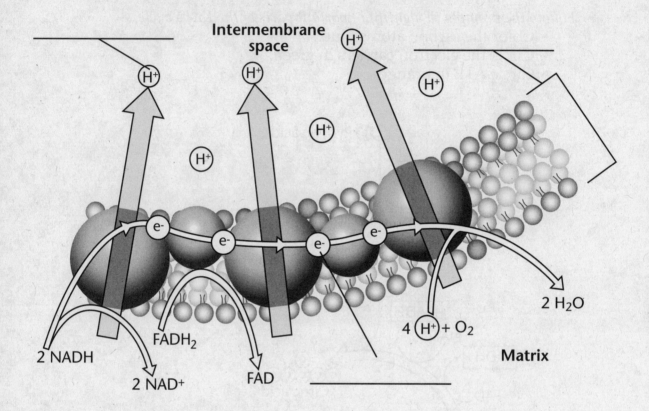

Use the diagram to answer the questions.

1. Where in the mitochondrion does the electron transport chain take place?

_____

_____

2. What happens to the high-energy electrons from the Krebs cycle?

_____

_____

Cellular Respiration and Photosynthesis

Cellular respiration and photosynthesis can be thought of as opposite processes. Energy flows in opposite directions in the two processes.

Complete the table using the words below. Some cells have been completed for you. Some words may be used more than once.

| carbon dioxide | energy release | mitochondria | water |

	Photosynthesis	Cellular Respiration
Function	energy capture	
Location	chloroplasts	
Reactants		glucose; oxygen
Products	oxygen; glucose	

Use the table to answer the questions.

1. Which process releases energy for the cell? Circle the correct answer.

   cellular respiration   photosynthesis

2. For which reaction is $6CO_2 + 6H_2O \rightarrow C_6H_{12}O_6 + 6O_2$ the correct equation? Circle the correct answer.

   cellular respiration   photosynthesis

3. How do the products of photosynthesis compare to the reactants of cellular respiration?

   _____

Chapter 9   Cellular Respiration

Vocabulary Review

Matching   *In the space provided, write the letter of the definition that best matches each term.*

_____ **1.** anaerobic

_____ **2.** aerobic

_____ **3.** calorie

_____ **4.** cellular respiration

a. process that releases energy by breaking down food in the presence of oxygen

b. amount of energy needed to raise the temperature of 1 g of water 1°C

c. chemical process that does not require oxygen

d. chemical process that requires oxygen

Matching   *In the space provided, write the letter of the definition that best matches each term.*

_____ **5.** fermentation

_____ **6.** glycolysis

_____ **7.** Krebs cycle

_____ **8.** NAD⁺

a. electron carrier of glycolysis

b. process that releases energy from food molecules when no oxygen is present

c. stage of cellular respiration in which pyruvic acid is broken down into carbon dioxide in a series of energy-extracting reactions

d. process in which glucose is broken down into two molecules of pyruvic acid

Summary

9–1 Chemical Pathways

Food serves as the source of energy for cells. Quite a lot of energy is stored in food. For instance, 1 gram of the sugar glucose releases 3811 calories of heat energy when burned in the presence of oxygen. A calorie is the amount of energy needed to raise the temperature of 1 gram of water 1 degree Celsius. Cells don't burn glucose and other food compounds. They gradually release the energy. The process begins with a pathway called glycolysis. In the presence of oxygen, glycolysis is followed by the Krebs cycle and the electron transport chain. Together, these three pathways make up cellular respiration. Cellular respiration is the process that releases energy by breaking down glucose and other food molecules in the presence of oxygen. The equation for cellular respiration is:

$$6O_2 + C_6H_{12}O_6 \rightarrow 6CO_2 + 6H_2O + \text{Energy}$$

$$\text{oxygen} + \text{glucose} \rightarrow \frac{\text{carbon}}{\text{dioxide}} + \text{water} + \text{energy}$$

There are three main stages of cellular respiration: (1) glycolysis, (2) the Krebs cycle, and (3) electron transport.

Glycolysis is the process in which one molecule of glucose is broken in half, producing two molecules of pyruvic acid, a 3-carbon compound. Through glycolysis, the cell gains 2 ATP molecules. In one of the reactions of glycolysis, the electron carrier NAD^+ accepts a pair of high-energy electrons, producing NADH. By doing this, NAD^+ helps pass energy from glucose to other pathways in the cell.

When oxygen is not present, glycolysis is followed by another pathway. This pathway is called fermentation. Fermentation releases energy from food molecules by producing ATP. Because fermentation does not require oxygen, it is said to be anaerobic.

During fermentation, cells convert NADH back into the electron carrier NAD^+, which is needed for glycolysis.

This action allows glycolysis to continue producing a steady supply of ATP. The two main types of fermentation are alcoholic fermentation and lactic acid fermentation. Yeasts and a few other microorganisms carry out alcoholic fermentation. The equation for alcoholic fermentation after glycolysis is:

$$\frac{\text{pyruvic}}{\text{acid}} + \text{NADH} \rightarrow \text{alcohol} + CO_2 + NAD^+$$

Lactic acid fermentation occurs in your muscles during rapid exercise. The equation for lactic acid fermentation after glycolysis is:

$$\text{pyruvic acid} + \text{NADH} \rightarrow \text{lactic acid} + NAD^+$$

9–2 The Krebs Cycle and Electron Transport

When oxygen is available, glycolysis is followed by the Krebs cycle and the electron transport chain. The three pathways together make up the process of cellular respiration. Because the pathways of cellular respiration require oxygen, they are said to be aerobic.

The Krebs cycle is the second stage of cellular respiration. In eukaryotes, the Krebs cycle takes place in the mitochondrion. During the Krebs cycle, pyruvic acid is broken down into carbon dioxide in a series of energy-extracting reactions. The Krebs cycle is also known as the citric acid cycle, because citric acid is one of the first products.

The Krebs cycle begins when pyruvic acid produced by glycolysis enters the mitochondrion. One carbon atom from pyruvic acid becomes part of a molecule of carbon dioxide, which is eventually released into the air. The carbon dioxide released during the Krebs cycle is the source of much of the carbon dioxide in air. The other two carbon atoms from pyruvic acid are used in a series of reactions. During these reactions, two energy carriers accept high-energy electrons. NAD^+ is changed to NADH, and FAD is changed to $FADH_2$. These molecules carry the high-energy electrons to the electron transport chain.

Electron transport is the third stage of cellular respiration. The electron transport chain uses the high-energy electrons from the Krebs cycle to convert ADP into ATP. In eukaryotes, the electron transport chain is composed of a series of carrier proteins located in the inner membrane of the mitochondrion. In prokaryotes, the same chain is in the cell membrane. In this pathway, high-energy electrons move from one carrier protein to the next. Their energy is used to move hydrogen ions across the membrane through a protein sphere called ATP synthase. Each time an ATP synthase spins, a phosphate group is added to an ADP molecule, producing an ATP molecule.

In the absence of oxygen, all the energy that a cell can extract from a single molecule of glucose is 2 ATP molecules—the product of glycolysis.

In the presence of oxygen, though, the cell can extract many more ATP molecules. The Krebs cycle and the electron transport chain enable the cell to produce 34 more ATP molecules per glucose molecule. The total, then, for cellular respiration (glycolysis plus the Krebs cycle plus electron transport) is 36 ATP molecules per glucose molecule.

Human body cells normally contain small amounts of ATP produced during cellular respiration. When the body needs energy in a hurry, muscle cells produce ATP by lactic acid fermentation. For long-term energy needs, the body must use cellular respiration.

The energy flows in photosynthesis and cellular respiration take place in opposite directions. On a global level, photosynthesis and cellular respiration are also opposites. Photosynthesis removes carbon dioxide from the atmosphere and puts back oxygen. Cellular respiration removes oxygen from the atmosphere and puts back carbon dioxide.

Chapter 9   Cellular Respiration

Section 9–1 Chemical Pathways (pages 221–225)

Key Concepts
- What is cellular respiration?
- What happens during the process of glycolysis?
- What are the two main types of fermentation?

Chemical Energy and Food (page 221)

1. What is a calorie? _____

_____

2. How many calories make up 1 Calorie? _____

3. Cellular respiration begins with a pathway called _____.

4. Is the following sentence true or false? Glycolysis releases a great amount of energy.

_____

Overview of Cellular Respiration (page 222)

5. What is cellular respiration? _____

_____

_____

6. What is the equation for cellular respiration, using chemical formulas?

_____

7. Label the three main stages of cellular respiration on the illustration of the complete process.

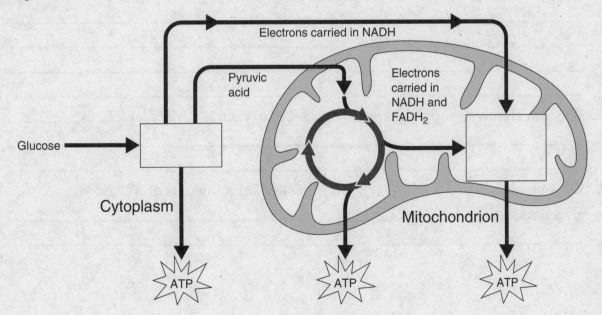

8. What would be the problem if cellular respiration took place in just one step?

_____

_____

_____

9. Where does glycolysis take place? _____

_____

_____

10. Where do the Krebs cycle and electron transport take place? _____

_____

Glycolysis (page 223)

11. What is glycolysis? _____

_____

_____

12. How does the cell get glycolysis going? _____

_____

13. If the cell uses 2 ATP molecules at the beginning of glycolysis, how does it end up with a net gain of 2 ATP molecules? _____

_____

_____

14. What is NAD^+? _____

_____

15. What is the function of NAD^+ in glycolysis? _____

_____

_____

_____

_____

16. Why can glycolysis supply energy to cells when oxygen is not available? _____

_____

_____

17. What problem does a cell have when it generates large amounts of ATP from glycolysis? _____

_____

_____

Fermentation (pages 224–225)

18. What is fermentation? _____
_____
_____

19. How does fermentation allow glycolysis to continue? _____
_____

20. Because fermentation does not require oxygen, it is said to be _____.

21. What are the two main types of fermentation?

   a. _____

   b. _____

22. What organisms use alcoholic fermentation? _____
_____

23. What is the equation for alcoholic fermentation after glycolysis?
_____

24. What happens to the small amount of alcohol produced in alcoholic fermentation
during the baking of bread? _____

25. What does lactic acid fermentation convert into lactic acid? _____
_____

26. What is the equation for lactic acid fermentation after glycolysis?
_____

27. During rapid exercise, how do your muscle cells produce ATP? _____
_____
_____

Reading Skill Practice

When you read about complex topics, writing an outline can help you organize
and understand the material. Outline Section 9–1 by using the headings and
subheadings as topics and subtopics and then writing the most important details
under each topic. Do your work on a separate sheet of paper.

Section 9–2 The Krebs Cycle and Electron Transport (pages 226–232)

🔑 Key Concepts

- What happens during the Krebs cycle?
- How are high-energy electrons used by the electron transport chain?

Introduction (page 226)

1. At the end of glycolysis, how much of the chemical energy in glucose is still unused?

_____

2. Because the final stages of cellular respiration require oxygen, they are said to be

_____.

The Krebs Cycle (pages 226–227)

3. In the presence of oxygen, how is the pyruvic acid produced in glycolysis used?

_____

_____

4. What happens to pyruvic acid during the Krebs cycle? _____

_____

_____

5. Why is the Krebs cycle also known as the citric acid cycle? _____

_____

_____

6. When does the Krebs cycle begin? _____

_____

7. What happens to each of the 3 carbon atoms in pyruvic acid when it is broken down?

_____

_____

_____

8. What happens to the carbon dioxide produced in breaking down pyruvic acid?

_____

9. How is citric acid produced? _____

_____

_____

10. During the energy extraction part of the Krebs cycle, how many molecules of CO_2 are released? _____

11. What is the energy tally from 1 molecule of pyruvic acid during the Krebs cycle?

_____

12. When electrons join NAD$^+$ and FAD during the Krebs cycle, what do they form?
_____

13. Why is the 4-carbon compound generated in the breakdown of citric acid the only permanent compound in the Krebs cycle? _____
_____
_____

Electron Transport (pages 228–229)

14. What is the electron transport chain? _____
_____

15. What does the electron transport chain use the high-energy electrons from the Krebs cycle for? _____
_____

16. How does the location of the electron transport chain differ in eukaryotes and prokaryotes? _____
_____
_____
_____

17. Where does the electron transport chain get the high-energy electrons that are passed down the chain? _____
_____
_____

18. Is the following sentence true or false? Hydrogen serves as the final electron acceptor of the electron transport chain. _____

19. What is the energy of the high-energy electrons used for every time 2 high-energy electrons move down the electron transport chain? _____
_____

20. What causes the H$^+$ ions in the intermembrane space to move through the channels in the membrane and out into the matrix? _____
_____
_____
_____
_____

21. On average, how many ATP molecules are produced as each pair of high-energy electrons moves down the electron transport chain? _____

22. Complete the flowchart about electron transport. (Review Figure 9–7 on page 228 of your textbook.)

High-energy electrons from NADH and FADH$_2$ are passed into and along the _____.

↓

The energy from the electrons moving down the chain is used to move H$^+$ ions across the _____.

↓

H$^+$ ions build up in the _____ space, making it _____ charged and making the matrix negatively charged.

↓

H$^+$ ions move through channels of _____ in the inner membrane.

↓

The ATP synthase uses the energy from the moving ions to combine ADP and phosphate, forming high-energy _____.

The Totals (page 229)

23. How many ATP molecules are formed during cellular respiration? _____

24. Why is more ATP generated from glucose in the presence of oxygen?

_____

_____

_____

_____

25. What happens to the energy of glucose that is not used to make ATP molecules?

_____

26. What are the final waste products of cellular respiration? _____

Energy and Exercise (pages 230–231)

27. What are three sources of ATP a human body uses at the beginning of a race?

_____

_____

_____

28. When a runner needs quick energy for a short race, what source can supply enough ATP for about 90 seconds? _____

29. Why does a sprinter have an oxygen debt to repay after the race is over? _____

_____

_____

_____

30. A runner needs more energy for a longer race. How does the body generate the necessary ATP? _____

31. Why are aerobic forms of exercise so beneficial for weight control? _____

_____

_____

_____

Comparing Photosynthesis and Cellular Respiration (page 232)

32. If photosynthesis is the process that "deposits" energy in a "savings account," then what is cellular respiration? _____

_____

33. How are photosynthesis and cellular respiration opposite in terms of carbon dioxide?

_____

_____

34. How are photosynthesis and cellular respiration opposite in terms of oxygen?

_____

_____

Vocabulary Review

Matching   *In the space provided, write the letter of the definition that best matches each term.*

_____ **1.** calorie

_____ **2.** glycolysis

_____ **3.** cellular respiration

_____ **4.** NAD⁺

_____ **5.** fermentation

_____ **6.** anaerobic

_____ **7.** aerobic

a. electron carrier

b. pathway that releases energy from food in the absence of oxygen

c. requires oxygen

d. process in which one molecule of glucose is broken in half, producing two molecules of pyruvic acid

e. does not require oxygen

f. amount of energy needed to raise 1 gram of water 1 degree Celsius

g. process that releases energy by breaking down food molecules in the presence of oxygen

Answering Questions   *In the space provided, write an answer to each question.*

8. What is the first stage of cellular respiration? _____

_____

9. What is the second stage of cellular respiration? _____

_____

10. What is the third stage of cellular respiration? _____

_____

11. How many ATP molecules can the cell produce from a single molecule of glucose

through glycolysis? _____

12. How many ATP molecules can the cell produce from a single molecule of glucose

through the complete process of cellular respiration? _____

Completion   *Write an equation for each of the pathways below.*

13. lactic acid fermentation after glycolysis _____

_____

14. alcoholic fermentation after glycolysis _____

_____

15. cellular respiration _____

_____

Name_____ Class_____ Date _____

Reviewing Key Concepts

Completion *On the lines provided, complete the following sentences.*

1. The process that releases energy by breaking down glucose and other food molecules in the presence of oxygen is called _____.

2. During glycolysis, one molecule of _____ is broken in half.

3. During glycolysis, NAD$^+$ is converted to _____.

4. Glycolysis produces a net gain of _____ ATP molecules for each reaction.

5. The products of alcoholic fermentation are _____, _____, and _____.

Short Answer *On the lines provided, answer the following questions.*

6. Why is fermentation considered an anaerobic process?

   _____

   _____

7. How does fermentation allow the production of ATP to continue?

   _____

   _____

Reviewing Key Skills

Labeling Diagrams *On the lines provided below, write the names of the substances in the glycolysis reaction that correspond to the numbers in the diagram.*

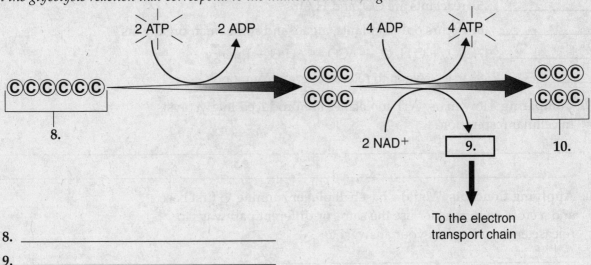

8. _____

9. _____

10. _____

Reviewing Key Concepts

Short Answer *On the lines provided, answer the following questions.*

1. How is pyruvic acid used in the Krebs cycle?

_____

_____

_____

2. How are glycolysis and cellular respiration related?

_____

_____

_____

3. What role do high-energy electrons play in the electron transport chain?

_____

_____

_____

4. What are the reactants in cellular respiration? What are the products?

_____

_____

_____

Reviewing Key Skills

Identification *On the lines provided, identify which phrase describes the following processes:* cellular respiration *or* photosynthesis.

_____ 5. reactants are CO_2 and H_2O

_____ 6. occurs only in plants, algae, and some microorganisms

_____ 7. $6O_2 + C_6H_{12}O_6 \rightarrow 6CO_2 + 6H_2O + Energy$

_____ 8. uses oxygen to release energy from food

9. **Comparing** How many ATP molecules are produced in glycolysis? In cellular respiration?

_____

_____

10. **Applying Concepts** Would a baseball player running to first base and a cross-country skier use the same or different pathways to release energy? Explain your answer.

_____

_____

_____

Chapter 9 Cellular Respiration — Chapter Vocabulary Review

Defining Terms *On the lines provided, write a definition for each of the following terms.*

1. calorie _____
_____

2. glycolysis _____
_____

3. cellular respiration _____
_____

4. NAD⁺ _____
_____

5. fermentation _____
_____

6. anaerobic _____
_____

7. aerobic _____
_____

8. Krebs cycle _____
_____

9. electron transport chain _____
_____

Identification *On the lines provided, identify which phrase describes the following processes:* cellular respiration, glycolysis, lactic acid fermentation, *or* alcoholic fermentation.

10. important in baking bread_____
_____

11. builds up in muscles after a few seconds of intense activity _____
_____

12. requires oxygen and glucose_____
_____

13. produces 2 ATP molecules and pyruvic acid _____
_____

14. almost the opposite process of photosynthesis _____
_____

15. the reason why runners breathe heavily after a race _____
_____

Name_____ Class_____ Date _____

Multiple Choice *On the lines provided, write the letter that best answers the question.*

_____ **16.** What is the net energy gain in glycolysis?
a. 4 molecules of ATP   c. 36 molecules of ATP
b. 2 molecules of ATP   d. 38 molecules of ATP

_____ **17.** Which of the following causes a painful, burning sensation in muscles after vigorous exercise?
a. alcohol   c. pyruvic acid
b. glycolysis   d. lactic acid

_____ **18.** What is another name for the Krebs cycle?
a. the glycolysis cycle   c. the citric acid cycle
b. alcoholic fermentation   d. the respiration cycle

Interpreting Diagrams *On the lines below, write the name of the stage of cellular respiration that corresponds with the numbers in the diagram.*

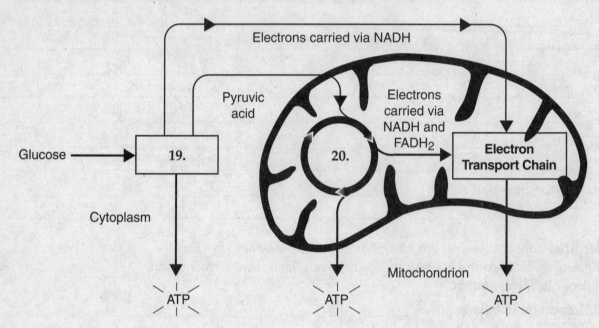

19. _____

20. _____

Lactobacillus

When was the last time your body benefited from lactic acid fermentation? Perhaps it was the last time your muscles needed a quick burst of energy. However, if you've recently enjoyed a cup of yogurt, a slice of cheese, or some kimchi or sauerkraut with your meal, you were eating the products of lactic acid fermentation.

Human muscle cells are not the only cells in which lactic acid fermentation occurs. In fact, there are countless organisms that take advantage of this process. Some of the most common lactic acid fermenting organisms are a group of bacteria called *Lactobacillus*. *Lactobacillus* uses lactic acid fermentation as one of its metabolic processes for producing energy. One of the byproducts of this process, lactic acid, is a useful ingredient in many foods.

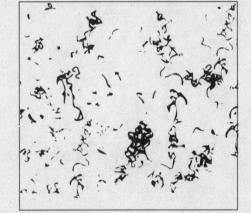

Lactobacillus **under a microscope**

Before the days of refrigeration, fresh food, especially milk, was good for only a matter of hours before it spoiled. Early people discovered, probably by accident, that fermented milk products such as yogurt would last for days or even weeks before it spoiled. The same is true for many other foods. How is this possible? The lactic acid produced by *Lactobacillus* inhibits the growth of other bacteria and organisms that could spoil the food.

Today, food spoilage is less of a concern than it was even a century ago. So why do people still eat foods fermented by *Lactobacillus*? Over the years, people learned to like the flavor of fermented foods. Lactic acid gives these foods a sour taste. If you've ever tried sour cream or buttermilk, you may be familiar with this taste, or even like it. Additionally, fermented milk products are high in calcium and protein, which makes them nutritious.

Evaluation *On a separate sheet of paper, answer the following questions.*

1. Suppose you lived over 100 years ago and you had a whole bowl of fresh milk but only one cup of yogurt left. Describe how you might make more yogurt.

2. How does lactic acid keep food from spoiling?

Chapter 9 Cellular Respiration   **Graphic Organizer**

Compare/Contrast Table

Compare glycolysis, fermentation, and cellular respiration by filling in the missing information in the compare/contrast table below. If there is not enough room in the table to write your answers, write them on a separate piece of paper.

	Glycolysis	Fermentation	Cellular Respiration
Function	1.	2.	3.
Reactants	4.	5.	Oxygen, glucose
Products	6.	NAD^+, alcohol, CO_2, lactic acid	7.
Advantages	Can produce thousands of ATP molecules in milliseconds	8.	9.
Disadvantages	10.	Produces ATP for only 20 or 30 seconds, lactic acid causes painful side effects	11.

Chapter 9 Cellular Respiration　　　　　　　　　　　**Chapter Test A**

Multiple Choice

Write the letter that best answers the question or completes the statement on the line provided.

____ 1. Which of the following is NOT a stage of cellular respiration?
　　a. fermentation　　　　　c. glycolysis
　　b. electron transport　　d. Krebs cycle

____ 2. What are the reactants in the equation for cellular respiration?
　　a. oxygen and lactic acid
　　b. carbon dioxide and water
　　c. glucose and oxygen
　　d. water and glucose

____ 3. The starting molecule for glycolysis is
　　a. ADP.　　　　　　　　c. citric acid.
　　b. pyruvic acid.　　　　d. glucose.

____ 4. One cause of muscle soreness is
　　a. alcoholic fermentation.
　　b. glycolysis.
　　c. lactic acid fermentation.
　　d. the Krebs cycle.

____ 5. Which process is used to produce beer and wine?
　　a. lactic acid fermentation
　　b. glycolysis
　　c. alcoholic fermentation
　　d. the Krebs cycle

____ 6. The conversion of pyruvic acid into lactic acid requires
　　a. alcohol.　　　　　　c. ATP.
　　b. oxygen.　　　　　　d. NADH.

____ 7. Which organism is NOT likely to carry out cellular respiration?
　　a. tree　　　　　　　　c. anaerobic bacterium
　　b. mushroom　　　　　d. tiger

____ 8. During one turn, the Krebs cycle produces
　　a. oxygen.　　　　　　c. electron carriers.
　　b. lactic acid.　　　　d. glucose.

____ 9. Which of the following passes high-energy electrons into the electron transport chain?
　　a. NADH and FADH$_2$　c. citric acid
　　b. ATP and ADP　　　　d. acetyl-CoA

_____10. Cellular respiration uses one molecule of glucose to produce
      a. 2 ATP molecules.   c. 36 ATP molecules.
      b. 34 ATP molecules.   d. 38 ATP molecules.

_____11. Breathing heavily after running a race is your body's way of
      a. making more citric acid.
      b. repaying an oxygen debt.
      c. restarting glycolysis.
      d. recharging the electron transport chain.

_____12. All of the following are sources of energy during exercise EXCEPT
      a. stored ATP.
      b. alcoholic fermentation.
      c. lactic acid fermentation.
      d. cellular respiration.

_____13. Which process does NOT release energy from glucose?
      a. glycolysis   c. fermentation
      b. photosynthesis   d. cellular respiration

_____14. Photosynthesis is to chloroplasts as cellular respiration is to
      a. chloroplasts.   c. mitochondria.
      b. cytoplasm.   d. nucleus.

_____15. Plants cannot release energy from glucose using
      a. glycolysis.   c. the Krebs cycle.
      b. photosynthesis.   d. cellular respiration.

Completion

Complete each statement on the line provided.

16. Cellular respiration occurs only in the presence of _____ .

17. Without oxygen, a cell can extract a net gain of only _____ molecules of ATP from each glucose molecule.

18. The pathway labeled B in Figure 1 is called _____ fermentation.

19. In Figure 1, only the pathway labeled _____ requires oxygen.

20. A high level of lactic acid in the blood is a sign that _____ fermentation has occurred.

Pathway A	Pathway B	Pathway C
Glucose	Glucose	Glucose
↓	↓	↓
Pyruvic acid	Pyruvic acid	Pyruvic acid
	↓	↓
	Carbon dioxide	Carbon dioxide
↓	+	+
Lactic acid	Ethyl alcohol	Water
+	+	+
2 ATP	2 ATP	36 ATP

Figure 1

Short Answer

In complete sentences, write the answers to the questions on the lines provided.

21. List the three main stages of cellular respiration in order. Where does each stage take place in the cell?

_____

_____

_____

22. What are the two types of fermentation? How do their products differ?

_____

_____

_____

23. Based on Figure 2, which type of fermentation does NOT give off carbon dioxide? Explain your answer.

_____

_____

_____

_____

Pathway A	**Pathway B**	**Pathway C**
Glucose	Glucose	Glucose
↓	↓	↓
Pyruvic acid	Pyruvic acid	Pyruvic acid
↓	↓	↓
	Carbon dioxide	Carbon dioxide
	+	+
Lactic acid	Ethyl alcohol	Water
+	+	+
2 ATP	2 ATP	36 ATP

Figure 2

24. What role does oxygen play in the electron transport chain?

_____

_____

_____

_____

25. What three sources of ATP does your body use during a long aerobic exercise session?

_____

_____

_____

Using Science Skills

Use the diagram on the next page to answer the following questions on the lines provided.

A scientist set up a respiration chamber as shown in Figure 3. She placed a mouse in flask B. Into flasks A, C, and D, she poured distilled water mixed with the acid-base indicator phenolphthalein. In the presence of CO_2, phenolphthalein turns from pink to clear. She allowed the mouse to stay in the chamber for about an hour.

Name_____ Class_____ Date _____

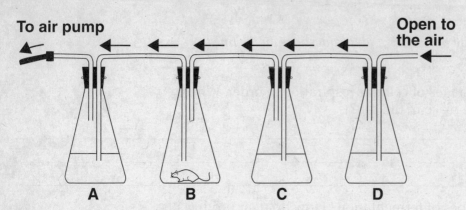

Figure 3

26. **Inferring** Write the equation for cellular respiration. Based on this equation and the setup shown in Figure 3, what substance(s) would you expect the mouse in flask B to give off?

_____

_____

_____

27. **Interpreting Graphics** What will the mouse require to carry out cellular respiration? Describe the flow of materials through the flasks in Figure 3. Will the mouse receive fresh air so that it can survive?

_____

_____

_____

_____

28. **Interpreting Graphics** Based on Figure 3, how will the scientist be able to detect whether the mouse is carrying out cellular respiration?

_____

_____

_____

29. **Applying Concepts** Assume that the scientist set up an identical respiration chamber, except that in this setup she placed a cricket in flask B instead of a mouse. At the end of one hour, she measured the amount of CO_2 given off by the cricket and the mouse. A small amount of CO_2 had been given off by the mouse, but little to no CO_2 had been given off by the cricket. Is the cricket undergoing cellular respiration? Explain these results.

_____

_____

_____

_____

30. Predicting Assume that the scientist set up an identical respiration chamber, except that in this setup she placed a mouse that had been exercising on a hamster wheel. Then, the scientist measured the amount of CO_2 given off by both mice at the end of 15 minutes. Predict which setup produced the most CO_2. Explain your answer.

_____

_____

_____

Essay

Write the answer to each question in the space provided.

31. List the main events of glycolysis. How many ATP molecules are produced and consumed by glycolysis? What effect does the presence of oxygen have on the events that follow glycolysis?

32. Compare lactic acid fermentation with alcoholic fermentation. Where does each process occur? What are the products of each process?

33. Identify the electron carriers of cellular respiration. Discuss the relationship between the electron carriers and the electron transport chain.

34. Explain how high-energy electrons are used by the electron transport chain.

35. Which pathways does the body use to release energy during exercise? Discuss these pathways in terms of a footrace.

Multiple Choice

Write the letter that best answers the question or completes the statement on the line provided.

_____ 1. Which of the following is released during cellular respiration?
    a. oxygen
    b. air
    c. energy

_____ 2. Cellular respiration releases energy by breaking down
    a. food molecules.
    b. ATP.
    c. carbon dioxide.

_____ 3. Which of these is a product of cellular respiration?
    a. oxygen
    b. water
    c. glucose

_____ 4. Which of these processes takes place in the cytoplasm of a cell?
    a. glycolysis
    b. electron transport
    c. Krebs cycle

_____ 5. Glycolysis provides a cell with a net gain of
    a. 2 ATP molecules.
    b. 4 ATP molecules.
    c. 18 ATP molecules.

_____ 6. Lactic acid fermentation occurs in
    a. bread dough.
    b. any environment containing oxygen.
    c. muscle cells.

_____ 7. The two main types of fermentation are called
    a. alcoholic and aerobic.
    b. aerobic and anaerobic.
    c. alcoholic and lactic acid.

_____ 8. In the presence of oxygen, glycolysis is followed by
    a. fermentation.
    b. photosynthesis.
    c. the Krebs cycle.

_____ 9. Cellular respiration is called an aerobic process because it requires
   a. light.
   b. exercise.
   c. oxygen.

_____ 10. The starting molecule for the Krebs cycle is
   a. glucose.
   b. NADH.
   c. pyruvic acid.

_____ 11. In eukaryotes, electron transport occurs in the
   a. mitochondria.
   b. chloroplasts.
   c. cell membrane.

_____ 12. The energy of the electrons passing along the electron transport chain is used to make
   a. lactic acid.
   b. ATP.
   c. alcohol.

_____ 13. When the body needs to exercise for longer than 90 seconds, it generates ATP by carrying out
   a. lactic acid fermentation.
   b. alcoholic fermentation.
   c. cellular respiration.

_____ 14. Unlike photosynthesis, cellular respiration occurs in
   a. animal cells only.
   b. plant cells only.
   c. all eukaryotic cells.

_____ 15. The products of photosynthesis are the
   a. products of cellular respiration.
   b. reactants of cellular respiration.
   c. products of glycolysis.

Completion

Complete each statement on the line provided.

16. Glycolysis converts glucose into two molecules of _____ .

17. The _____ is a series of carrier proteins.

18. The body gets rid of lactic acid in a chemical pathway that requires _____ .

19. Based on Figure 1, _____ ATP molecules are formed by fermentation.

20. Based on Figure 1, the complete breakdown of glucose through cellular respiration results in the production of _____ ATP molecules.

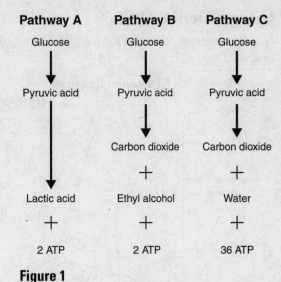

Figure 1

Short Answer

In complete sentences, write the answers to the questions on the lines provided.

21. What is cellular respiration?

_____

_____

22. What happens during glycolysis?

_____

_____

23. Why is the Krebs cycle also known as the citric acid cycle?

_____

_____

24. What is the main function of the electron transport chain?

_____

_____

25. What roles does oxygen play in photosynthesis and in cellular respiration?

_____

_____

_____

Using Science Skills

Use the diagram below to answer the following questions on the lines provided.

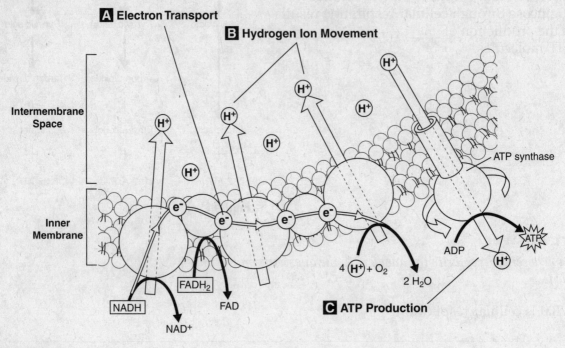

Figure 2

26. Interpreting Graphics What process does Figure 2 show?

_____

27. Interpreting Graphics Look at Figure 2. Where do the electrons moving along the inner membrane come from?

_____

_____

28. Interpreting Graphics Where do the electrons moving along the inner membrane in Figure 2 end up?

_____

29. Inferring Look at the arrows and H⁺ ions in Figure 2. Which direction do most of the H⁺ ions move in? What is the result of this movement?

_____

_____

_____

30. Interpreting Graphics ATP synthase is an enzyme. Find ATP synthase in Figure 2. What reaction does ATP synthase catalyze when an H⁺ ion passes through its channel?

_____

_____

LESSON PLAN 10–1 (pages 241–243)

Cell Growth

Time
1 period
1/2 block

Section Objectives
Local Standards

- **10.1.1 Explain** the problems that growth causes for cells.
- **10.1.2 Describe** how cell division solves the problems of cell growth.

Vocabulary cell division

---

1 FOCUS

Reading Strategy
Students preview Figure 10–2 and explain the implications for cell size and growth.

Targeted Resources
- ❑ Transparencies: **135** Section 10–1 Interest Grabber
- ❑ Transparencies: **136** Section 10–1 Outline

---

2 INSTRUCT

Build Science Skills: Drawing Conclusions
Groups of students measure boxes and reach conclusions about how volume and surface area increases with box size. **L2** **L3**

Quick Lab
Students use a model to explain why a cell cannot grow indefinitely. **L2**

Make Connections: Mathematics
Review what a ratio is and how ratios are expressed. **L1** **L2**

Use Visuals: Figure 10–2
Use Figure 10–2 to reinforce an understanding of ratio of surface area to volume in cells. **L2**

Targeted Resources
- ❑ Reading and Study Workbook: Section 10–1
- ❑ Adapted Reading and Study Workbook: Section 10–1
- ❑ Teaching Resources: Section Summaries 10–1, Worksheets 10–1
- ❑ Transparencies: **137** Ratio of Surface Area to Volume in Cells
- ❑ **PHSchool.com** Cell growth

---

3 ASSESS

Evaluate Understanding
Students write a paragraph that explains why a human cell never grows as large as a fist.

Reteach
Students calculate ratios of surface area to volume for a cell that doubles in size.

Targeted Resources
- ❑ Teaching Resources: Section Review 10–1
- ❑ 〈 **iText** 〉 Section 10–1

LESSON PLAN 10–2 (pages 244–249)

Cell Division

Section Objectives

Local Standards

- **10.2.1 Name** the main events of the cell cycle.
- **10.2.2 Describe** what happens during the four phases of mitosis.

Vocabulary mitosis • cytokinesis • chromatid • centromere • interphase • cell cycle • prophase • centriole • spindle • metaphase • anaphase • telophase

1 FOCUS

Reading Strategy

Students write a summary of the information in Figure 10–5 and then revise the summary as they read.

Targeted Resources

❏ Transparencies: **138** Section 10–2 Interest Grabber

❏ Transparencies: **139** Section 10–2 Outline

❏ Transparencies: **140** Concept Map

2 INSTRUCT

Demonstration

Use pipe cleaners and a pin to reinforce understanding of chromatids and centromeres. **L1 L2**

Build Science Skills: Using Models

Groups plan and create a large four-frame cartoon that tells the story of the cell cycle. **L2**

Use Visuals: Figure 10–5

Use Figure 10–5 to review events in the four phases of mitosis. **L2**

Build Science Skills: Using Models

Students manipulate models of cells as volunteers explain what occurs during each phase of mitosis. **L1 L2**

Analyzing Data

Students analyze life spans of various human cells. **L2 L3**

Targeted Resources

❏ Reading and Study Workbook: Section 10–2

❏ Adapted Reading and Study Workbook: Section 10–2

❏ Transparencies: **141** Figure 10–4 The Cell Cycle, **142** Figure 10–5 Mitosis and Cytokinesis

❏ Teaching Resources: Section Summaries 10–2, Worksheets 10–2, Enrichment

❏ Lab Worksheets: Chapter 10 Exploration

❏ Lab Manual A: Chapter 10 Lab

❏ Lab Manual B: Chapter 10 Lab

❏ **NSTA** *SciLINKS* Cell cycle

3 ASSESS

Evaluate Understanding

Call on students to explain events of the cell cycle, using Figure 10–4 as a reference.

Reteach

Students make a flowchart of what occurs during cell division.

Targeted Resources

❏ Teaching Resources: Section Review 10–2

❏ **iText** Section 10–2

LESSON PLAN 10–3 (pages 250–252)

Regulating the Cell Cycle

Time
1 period
1/2 block

Section Objectives
Local Standards

- **10.3.1 Identify** a factor that can stop cells from growing.
- **10.3.2 Describe** how the cell cycle is regulated.
- **10.3.3 Explain** how cancer cells are different from other cells.

Vocabulary cyclin • cancer

1 FOCUS

Vocabulary Preview
Have students divide the Vocabulary words into separate syllables.

Targeted Resources
❑ Transparencies: **143** Section 10–3 Interest Grabber
❑ Transparencies: **144** Section 10–3 Outline

2 INSTRUCT

Use Visuals: Figure 10–7
Use Figure 10–7 to review controls on cell division. **L1** **L2**

Use Visuals: Figure 10–8
Use Figure 10–8 to reinforce concepts related to cell cycle regulators. **L2**

Build Science Skills: Designing Experiments
Students design experiments to test a hypothesis about cell cycle regulators. **L2** **L3**

Use Community Resources
Invite someone from a local cancer support group to address the class about the causes, symptoms, and treatments of cancer. **L2**

Targeted Resources
❑ Reading and Study Workbook: Section 10–3
❑ Adapted Reading and Study Workbook: Section 10–3
❑ Teaching Resources: Section Summaries 10–3, Worksheets 10–3
❑ Transparencies: **145** Control of Cell Division, **146** Figure 10–8 Effect of Cyclins
❑ BioDetectives DVD: "Skin Cancer: Deadly Cells"
❑ Investigations in Forensics: Investigation 3

3 ASSESS

Evaluate Understanding
Call on students to explain what controls cell division, what regulates the cell cycle, and the nature of cancer cells.

Reteach
Students write a public-health pamphlet explaining cell division and cancer.

Targeted Resources
❑ Teaching Resources: Section Review 10–3, Chapter Vocabulary Review, Graphic Organizer, Chapter 10 Tests: Levels A and B
❑ Lab Assessment: Laboratory Assessment 3
❑  Section 10–3, Chapter 10 Assessment
❑ **PHSchool.com** Online Chapter 10 Test

Chapter 10   Cell Growth and Division

Summary

10–1 Cell Growth

In most cases, living things grow by producing more cells. There are two main reasons why cells divide:

1. **The larger a cell gets, the more demands it places on its DNA.**

2. **As a cell gets larger, it has more trouble moving enough nutrients (food) and wastes across its cell membrane.** The rates at which materials move through the cell membrane depend on the cell's surface area—the total area of its cell membrane. However, the rate at which food and oxygen are used up and waste products are formed depends on the cell's volume. As a cell grows, its volume increases faster than its surface area. That is, as a cell becomes larger, its ratio of surface area to volume decreases.

Before a cell gets too large, it divides, forming two "daughter" cells. **Cell division** is the process by which a cell divides into two new daughter cells.

10–2 Cell Division

A cell must copy its genetic information before cell division begins. Each daughter cell then gets a complete copy of that information.

- In most prokaryotes, the rest of cell division is a simple matter of separating the contents of the cell into two parts.
- In eukaryotes, cell division occurs in two main stages, mitosis and cytokinesis. **Mitosis** is the division of the nucleus. **Cytokinesis** is the division of the cytoplasm.

The **cell cycle** is a series of events cells go through as they grow and divide. **During the cell cycle, a cell grows, prepares for division, and divides to form two daughter cells. Each daughter cell then begins the cycle again.** The phases of the cell cycle include interphase and cell division.

- **Interphase** is divided into three phases: G_1, S, and G_2.
  - During the G_1 phase, cells increase in size and make new proteins and organelles.
  - In the S phase, replication (copying) of chromosomes takes place.
  - During the G_2 phase, many of the organelles and molecules needed for cell division are produced.
- The M phase, or cell division includes mitosis and cytokinesis.

Biologists divide the events of mitosis into four phases: prophase, metaphase, anaphase, and telophase.

1. **Prophase.** During prophase, the chromosomes condense and become visible. There are two tiny structures located in the cytoplasm near the nuclear envelope. These structures are called centrioles. The centrioles separate and move to opposite sides of the nucleus. The spindle is a structure that helps move chromosomes apart. During prophase, the chromosomes attach to fibers in the spindle. At the end of prophase, the nuclear envelope breaks down.

2. **Metaphase.** During metaphase, chromosomes line up across the center of the cell. The centromere of each chromosome attaches to the spindle.

3. **Anaphase.** During anaphase, the centromeres joining the sister chromatids split. The sister chromotids become individual chromosomes. The two sets of chromosomes move apart.

4. **Telophase.** During telophase, the chromosomes move to opposite ends of the cell. They lose their distinct shapes. Two new nuclear envelopes form.

Cytokinesis usually occurs at the same time as telophase. In most animal cells, the cell membrane pinches the cytoplasm into two nearly equal parts. In plant cells, a cell plate forms midway between the divided nuclei. A cell wall then begins to form in the cell plate.

10–3 Regulating the Cell Cycle

In a multicellular organism, cell growth and cell division are carefully controlled. For instance, when an injury such as a cut in the skin occurs, cells at the edge of the cut divide rapidly. When the healing process is nearly complete, the rate of cell division slows and then returns to normal.

Cyclins—a group of proteins—regulate the timing of the cell cycle in eukaryotic cells. Cyclins are one group of proteins involved in cell cycle regulation. Other proteins, called regulatory proteins, regulate the cell cycle in different ways.

Controls on cell growth can be turned on and off by the body. **Cancer** is a disorder in which some of the body's cells lose the ability to control growth. **Cancer cells do not respond to the signals that control the growth of most cells.** As a result, cancer cells divide uncontrollably. Cancer cells do not stop growing when they touch other cells. Instead, they continue to grow and divide until their supply of nutrients is used up.

Surface Area and Volume

Use what you know about surface area and volume to complete the table.

Cell	1 cm ... 1 cm 1 cm	3 cm ... 3 cm 3 cm
What is the surface area? (length × width × 6)	__ cm × __ cm × 6 = __ cm²	__ cm × __ cm × 6 = __ cm²
What is the volume? (length × width × height)	__ cm × __ cm × __ cm = __ cm³	__ cm × __ cm × __ cm = __ cm³

Use the table to answer the questions.

1. Suppose you had enough smaller cells to fill the larger cell. What would their combined surface area be?

   _____ smaller cells × _____ cm² for one cell =

   _____ cm² total

2. Which has a greater surface area? Circle the best answer.

   one large cell   27 smaller cells

Cell Cycle

Cell growth and division occur in a regular cycle. This cycle is divided into four phases: G_1, S, G_2, and M. The diagram shows this cycle, along with events that occur in each phase.

Follow the prompts below.
- Color the phase in which most cell growth occurs blue.
- Color the phase in which DNA replication occurs red.
- Color the phase in which preparation for mitosis occurs yellow.
- Color the phase in which mitosis and cytokinesis occur orange.

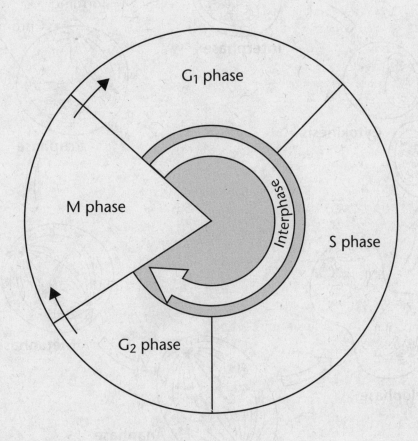

Use the diagram to answer the questions.

1. Which three phases make up interphase?

_____

2. Many organelles and molecules needed for cell division are formed after DNA replication and before mitosis. In which phase are they formed?

_____

Mitosis

Mitosis is the process by which the nucleus of most eukaryotic cells divides. Mitosis has four phases: prophase, metaphase, anaphase, and telophase.

Color each chromosome in prophase a different color. Follow each of these chromosomes through mitosis. Show this by coloring the correct structures in each phase of mitosis.

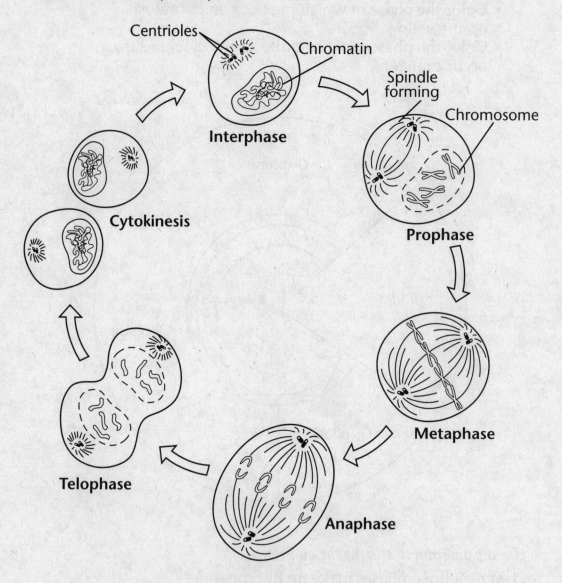

Use the diagram to answer the questions.

1. In which phase do the chromosomes line up in the middle of

   the cell? _____

2. In which process are two daughter cells formed?

   _____

Cytokinesis

Cytokinesis is the final step of cell division. During cytokinesis in plant cells, a cell plate forms between the two daughter cells.

The diagram shows plant cytokinesis in progress.

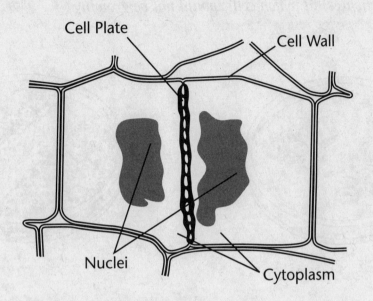

In the space provided below, draw how the cells will look when cytokinesis is complete.

Use the diagram to answer the questions. Circle the correct answer.

1. What structure forms in the cell plate?

    cell wall   cytoplasm

2. What divides during cytokinesis?

    cytoplasm   nucleus

Controls on Cell Division

When cells come in contact with one another, molecules on their surfaces signal them to stop growing. This prevents cells from growing uncontrollably and disrupting nearby tissues.

Circle the dish(es) in which cells would be stimulated to grow. Mark an X over the dish(es) in which cells would not be growing.

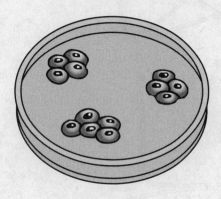

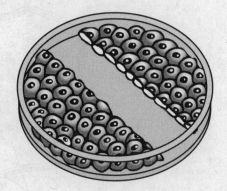

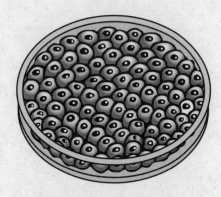

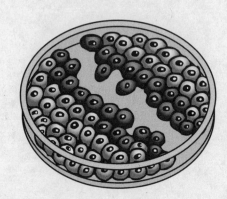

Answer the questions.

1. What happens when there is a gap between two groups of cells?

_____

2. Which of the following best describes cancer? Circle the correct answer.

uncontrolled cell growth   cells stop growing

Chapter 10   Cell Growth and Division

Vocabulary Review

True or False   *If the statement is true, write* true. *If it is false, write* false.

_____ **1.** One of two identical "sister" parts of a copied chromosome is called a chromatid.

_____ **2.** The final phase of mitosis in which the nuclear envelope re-forms is called anaphase.

_____ **3.** Division of the cytoplasm takes place during prophase.

_____ **4.** A disorder in which some of the body's cells grow uncontrollably is called cancer.

_____ **5.** The first phase of mitosis is called prophase.

_____ **6.** The part of the cell cycle in which the cell grows and replicates its DNA is interphase.

_____ **7.** The third stage of mitosis during which the sister chromatids separate and become individual chromosomes is cytokinesis.

_____ **8.** The division of the cell nucleus occurs during interphase.

_____ **9.** A tiny structure located in the cytoplasm near the nuclear envelope is a centriole.

_____ **10.** The stage of mitosis in which the chromo-somes line up across the center of the cell is metaphase.

| Chapter 10   Cell Growth and Division |

Summary

10–1 Cell Growth

The larger a cell becomes, the more demands the cell places on its DNA. As a cell increases in size, it usually does not make copies of DNA. If a cell were to grow without limit, an "information crisis" would occur. In addition, as a cell increases in size, the more trouble it has moving enough nutrients (food) and wastes across its cell membrane. The rate at which materials move through the cell membrane depends on the surface area of the cell—the total area of its cell membrane. However, the rate at which food and oxygen are used up and waste products are produced depends on the volume of the cell.

If a cell were a cube, you could determine surface area by multiplying length × width × number of sides. You could determine volume by multiplying length × width × height. You then could determine the cell's ratio of surface area to volume by dividing the surface area by the volume. As a cell grows, its volume increases more rapidly than its surface area. That is, as a cell becomes larger, its ratio of surface area to volume decreases.

Before a cell becomes too large, a growing cell divides, forming two "daughter" cells. The process by which a cell divides into two new daughter cells is called cell division.

10–2 Cell Division

Each cell has only one set of genetic information. For that reason, a cell must first copy its genetic information before cell division begins. Each daughter cell then gets a complete copy of that information. In most prokaryotes, cell division is a simple matter of separating the contents of the cell into two parts. In eukaryotes, cell division occurs in two main stages. The first stage is division of the nucleus, called mitosis. The second stage is division of the cytoplasm, called cytokinesis.

In eukaryotes, genetic information is passed on by chromosomes. Well before cell division, each chromosome is replicated (copied). When copying occurs, each chromosome consists of two identical "sister" chromatids. Each pair of chromatids is attached at an area called a centromere.

The cell cycle is a series of events that cells go through as they grow and divide. During the cell cycle, a cell grows, prepares for division, and divides to form two daughter cells, each of which then begins the cycle again. The cell cycle consists of four phases. The M phase includes mitosis and cytokinesis. The other three phases are sometimes grouped together and called interphase. Interphase is divided into three phases: G_1, S, and G_2. During the G_1 phase, cells increase in size and make new proteins and organelles. During the next phase, the S phase, the replication (copying) of chromosomes takes place. When the S phase is complete, the cell enters the G_2 phase. During the G_2 phase, many of the organelles and molecules required for cell division are produced.

Mitosis consists of four phases: prophase, metaphase, anaphase, and telophase. The first and longest phase is prophase. During prophase, the chromosomes condense and become visible. The centrioles separate and take up positions on opposite sides of the nucleus. Centrioles are two tiny structures located in the cytoplasm near the nuclear envelope. The centrioles lie in a region called the centrosome that helps to organize the spindle, a fanlike microtubule structure that helps separate the chromosomes.

During the second phase, called metaphase, chromosomes line up across the center of the cell. During the third phase, called anaphase, the centromeres that join the sister chromatids split and the sister chromatids become individual chromosomes. The two sets of chromosomes move apart. During the fourth and final phase, called telophase, the chromosomes gather at opposite ends of the cell and lose their distinct shapes. Two new nuclear envelopes form.

Cytokinesis usually occurs at the same time as telophase. In most animal cells, the cell membrane is drawn inward until the cytoplasm is pinched into two nearly equal parts. In plant cells, a structure known as a cell plate forms midway between the divided nuclei. A cell wall then begins to appear in the cell plate.

10–3 Regulating the Cell Cycle

In a multicellular organism, cell growth and cell division are carefully controlled. For instance, when an injury such as a cut in the skin occurs, cells at the edge of the cut will divide rapidly. When the healing process nears completion, the rate of cell division slows down and then returns to normal.

Cyclins—a group of proteins—regulate the timing of the cell cycle in eukaryotic cells. There are two types of these regulatory proteins: internal regulators and external regulators.

Internal regulators are proteins that respond to events inside the cell. They allow the cell cycle to proceed only when certain processes have happened inside the cell. External regulators are proteins that respond to events outside the cell. They direct cells to speed up or slow down the cell cycle. Growth factors are important external regulators. Growth factors stimulate growth and division of cells, such as during the development of the embryo or when a wound is healing.

Cancer is a disorder in which some of the body's own cells lose the ability to control growth. Cancer cells do not respond to the signals that regulate the growth of most cells. As a result, they divide uncontrollably and form masses of cells called tumors. Cancer cells may break lose from tumors and spread throughout the body. Cancer cells damage tissues and disrupt normal activities, causing serious medical problems or even death.

Section 10–1 Cell Growth (pages 241–243)

👄 **Key Concept**
- What problems does growth cause for cells?

Limits to Cell Growth (pages 241–243)

1. What are two reasons why cells divide rather than continue to grow indefinitely?

   a. _____

   _____

   b. _____

   _____

   _____

2. Is the following sentence true or false? As a cell increases in size, it usually makes extra copies of its DNA. _____

3. Circle the letter of what determines the rate at which food and oxygen in a cell are used up and waste products produced.

   a. The cell's organelles   c. The cell's location

   b. The cell's volume   d. The cell's DNA

4. How can you obtain a cell's ratio of surface area to volume? _____

   _____

5. If a cell's surface area is 6 cm^3 and its volume is 1 cm^3, then what is its ratio of surface area to volume? _____

6. Is the following sentence true or false? As a cell grows in size, its volume increases much more rapidly than its surface area. _____

7. Circle the letter of what happens to a cell's ratio of surface area to volume as the cell's volume increases more rapidly than its surface area.

   a. The ratio decreases.   c. The ratio remains the same.

   b. The ratio increases.   d. The ratio disappears.

Division of the Cell (page 243)

8. What is cell division? _____

   _____

   _____

9. How does cell division solve the problem of increasing size? _____

   _____

   _____

Section 10–2 Cell Division (pages 244–249)

🔑 Key Concepts
- What are the main events of the cell cycle?
- What are the four phases of mitosis?

Chromosomes (pages 244–245)

1. In eukaryotic cells, what are the two main stages of cell division? _____

   _____

2. When chromosomes become visible at the beginning of cell division, what does each

   chromosome consist of? _____

   _____

3. Each pair of chromatids is attached at an area called the _____.

The Cell Cycle (page 245)

4. The period of growth in between cell divisions is called _____.

5. What is the cell cycle? _____

   _____

   _____

6. Complete the diagram of the cell cycle by writing the names of each
   of the four phases.

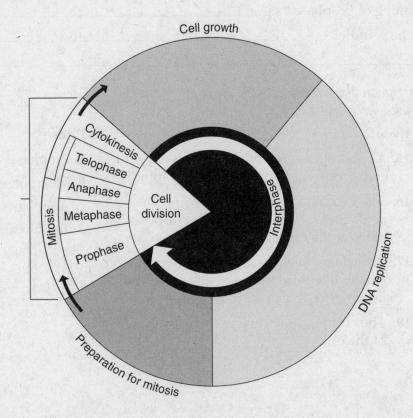

7. The division of the cell nucleus during the M phase of the cell cycle is called
   _____.

Events of the Cell Cycle (page 245)

8. Interphase is divided into what three phases?

   a. _____ b. _____ c. _____

9. What happens during the G_1 phase? _____
   _____
   _____

10. What happens during the S phase? _____
    _____
    _____

11. What happens during the G_2 phase? _____
    _____
    _____

Mitosis (pages 246–248)

12. What are the four phases of mitosis?

    a. _____   c. _____

    b. _____   d. _____

13. What are the two tiny structures located in the cytoplasm near the nuclear envelope at
    the beginning of prophase? _____

14. What is the spindle? _____
    _____

*Match the description of the event with the phase of mitosis it is in. Each
phase may be used more than once.*

Event	Phase
_____ 15. The chromosomes move until they form two groups near the poles of the spindle.	a. Prophase
_____ 16. The chromosomes become visible. The centrioles take up positions on opposite sides of the nucleus.	b. Metaphase
_____ 17. A nuclear envelope re-forms around each cluster of chromosomes. The nucleolus becomes visible in each daughter nucleus.	c. Anaphase
_____ 18. The chromosomes line up across the center of the cell.	d. Telophase

19. Identify each of the four phases of mitosis pictured below.

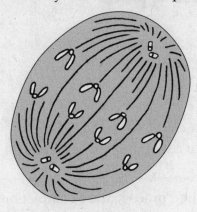

a. _____

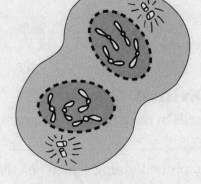

c. _____

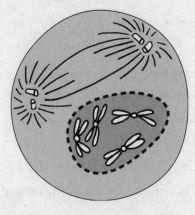

b. _____

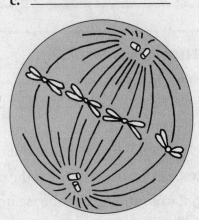

d. _____

Cytokinesis (page 248)

20. What is cytokinesis? _____

21. How does cytokinesis occur in most animal cells? _____

_____

22. What forms midway between the divided nucleus during cytokinesis in plant cells?

_____

Reading Skill Practice

You may sometimes forget the meanings of the vocabulary terms that were introduced earlier in the textbook. When this happens, you can check the meanings of the terms in the Glossary, which you can find at the end of the book, preceding the Index. Use the Glossary to review the meanings of all the vocabulary terms listed on page 244. Write their definitions on a separate sheet of paper.

Section 10–3 Regulating the Cell Cycle
(pages 250–252)

⬤ Key Concepts
- How is the cell cycle regulated?
- How are cancer cells different from other cells?

Controls on Cell Division (page 250)

1. What happens to the cells at the edges of an injury when a cut in the skin or a break in a bone occurs? _____

2. What happens to the rapidly dividing cells when the healing process nears completion? _____
_____

Cell Cycle Regulators (page 251)

3. What do cyclins regulate? _____
_____

4. What are internal regulators? _____

5. Circle the letter of each sentence that is true about external regulators.

    a. They direct cells to speed up or slow down the cell cycle.

    b. They prevent the cell from entering anaphase until all its chromosomes are attached to the mitotic spindle.

    c. They include growth factors.

    d. They prevent excessive cell growth and keep the tissues of the body from disrupting one another.

Uncontrolled Cell Growth (page 252)

6. What is cancer? _____
_____

7. Complete the flowchart about cancer.

Cancer cells don't respond to signals that regulate _____ .

↓

Cancer cells form masses of cells called _____ .

↓

Cancer cells break loose and spread throughout the _____ .

Chapter 10   Cell Growth and Division

Vocabulary Review

Completion   *Fill in the blanks with terms from Chapter 10.*

1. The division of a cell's cytoplasm is called _____.

2. The final phase of mitosis is _____.

3. The phase of mitosis in which microtubules connect the centromere of each chromosome to the poles of the spindle is _____.

4. At the beginning of cell division, each chromosome consists of two sister _____.

5. The longest phase of mitosis is _____.

6. The phase of mitosis that ends when the chromosomes stop moving is _____.

7. The process by which a cell divides into two new daughter cells is called _____.

8. A tiny structure located in the cytoplasm near the nuclear envelope is a(an) _____.

9. A disorder in which some of the body's cells lose the ability to control growth is called _____.

10. The area where a pair of chromatids is attached is the _____.

11. The division of the cell nucleus is called _____.

12. A protein that regulates the timing of the cell cycle in eukaryotic cells is _____.

13. The series of events that cells go through as they grow and divide is known as the _____.

14. A fanlike microtubule structure that helps separate the chromosomes is a(an) _____.

15. The time period between cell divisions is called _____.

Chapter 10 Cell Growth and Division   Section Review 10-1

Reviewing Key Concepts

Completion *On the lines provided, complete the following sentences.*

1. The larger the cell, the more trouble it has moving enough nutrients and
   wastes across the _____.

2. As the length of a cell increases, its volume increases faster than its
   _____.

3. To avoid growing too large, cells regulate their size by
   _____.

Short Answer *On the lines provided, answer the following questions.*

4. What can happen if a cell were to get too large for the amount of
   DNA it has?

   _____

   _____

5. What substances must pass through a cell's membrane for the cell to
   continue to function?

   _____

   _____

6. How does a cell's ratio of surface area to volume change as the cell
   grows larger?

   _____

   _____

7. Why do cells divide?

   _____

   _____

Reviewing Key Skills

Calculating *Complete the following table.*

Cell	Surface Area	Volume	Ratio of Surface Area to Volume
1	42 cm^2	8. _____	7:1
2	78 cm^2	13 cm^3	9. _____
3	10. _____	16 cm^3	5:1

Chapter 10 Cell Growth and Division

Reviewing Key Concepts

Short Answer *On the lines provided, answer the following questions.*

1. What are the four phases of the cell cycle?

   _____

   _____

2. What happens when the cell copies its chromosomes?

   _____

3. What happens during cytokinesis?

   _____

Classifying *On the line provided, label each event with one of the four phases of mitosis in which it occurs. A phase may be used more than once.*

_____ 4. The chromosomes line up across the middle of the cell.

_____ 5. Chromosomes become visible.

_____ 6. Centrioles separate.

_____ 7. Sister chromatids separate into individual chromosomes.

_____ 8. Two new nuclear envelopes form.

_____ 9. The nucleolus disappears and the nuclear envelope breaks down.

_____ 10. Each chromosome is connected to a spindle fiber.

_____ 11. The individual chromosomes move apart.

Reviewing Key Skills

12. **Applying Concepts** Explain why the terms *cell division* and *mitosis* should not be used interchangeably.

    _____

    _____

13. **Calculating** If a particular type of cell completes one cell cycle in 75 minutes, and you start with one cell, how many cells would be present after 7.5 hours?

    _____

14. **Inferring** Many plant cells have more than two complete sets of chromosomes in each cell. Explain how this might occur.

    _____

    _____

15. **Comparing and Contrasting** How does an animal cell differ from a plant cell during cell division?

    _____

    _____

Chapter 10 Cell Growth and Division   **Section Review 10-3**

Reviewing Key Concepts

Short Answer *On the lines provided, answer the following questions.*

1. What is the function of cyclin in eukaryotic cells?

   _____

   _____

2. Explain the importance of internal regulators.

   _____

   _____

3. How do external regulators respond to events outside the cell?

   _____

   _____

4. What causes the abnormal growth of cancer cells?

   _____

   _____

Reviewing Key Skills

5. **Applying Concepts** Do all cells in the body have the same growth rate? Give examples.

   _____

   _____

6. **Posing Questions** Cyclin seems to regulate the cell cycle. What questions might scientists have asked following the discovery of cyclin?

   _____

   _____

7. **Comparing and Contrasting** What are the similarities and the differences between internal and external cell cycle regulators?

   _____

   _____

8. **Inferring** Describe a situation in the human body that would cause an increase in the rate of cell division of certain cells, followed by a return to the normal rate of division.

   _____

   _____

   _____

   _____

Chapter 10 Cell Growth and Division   Chapter Vocabulary Review

Completion *On the lines provided, complete the following sentences.*

1. The process by which a cell divides into two daughter cells is _____.

2. Each pair of chromatids is attached at an area called the

   _____.

3. The three phases of _____ are G_1, S, and G_2.

4. The _____ is the series of events that cells go through as they grow and divide.

5. The _____ is a fanlike microtubule structure that helps separate the chromosomes.

6. _____ is the division of the cell nucleus.

7. The four phases of mitosis are _____,

   _____, _____, and

   _____.

8. The division of the cytoplasm during the M phase is called

   _____.

9. Proteins known as _____ regulate the timing of the cell cycle in eukaryotic cells .

10. _____ is a disorder in which some of the body's own cells lose the ability to control growth.

Multiple Choice *On the line provided, write the letter that best completes the statements or answers the question.*

_____ 11. What process ensures that each daughter cell gets one complete set of genetic information and that each daughter cell also has increased surface area?
   a. cell division   c. cytokinesis
   b. mitosis   d. cancer

_____ 12. Before cell division, each chromosome consists of two identical "sister"
   a. centromeres.   c. chromatids.
   b. cell cycles.   d. spindles.

_____ 13. The four phases of the cell cycle are
   a. interphase, mitosis, G_1, and G_2.
   b. M phase, G_1 phase, S phase, and G_2 phase.
   c. prophase, metaphase, anaphase, and telophase.
   d. cytokinesis, mitosis, interphase, and metaphase.

_____ 14. What phase of mitosis takes the longest period of time?
   a. prophase   c. anaphase
   b. cytokinesis   d. interphase

_____ **15.** The two small structures that separate and take up
positions on opposite sides of the nucleus during
prophase are the
a. centrioles.   c. chromatids.
b. centromeres.   d. spindles.

_____ **16.** What phase of mitosis usually occurs at the same
time as cytokinesis?
a. anaphase   c. prophase
b. telophase   d. cell division

_____ **17.** What is the name for tumors that form and can
cause damage to surrounding tissue?
a. cyclins   c. cytokinesis
b. mitosis   d. cancer

Labeling Diagrams *On the lines below, label the events in the cell cycle that*
correspond with the numbers in the diagram.

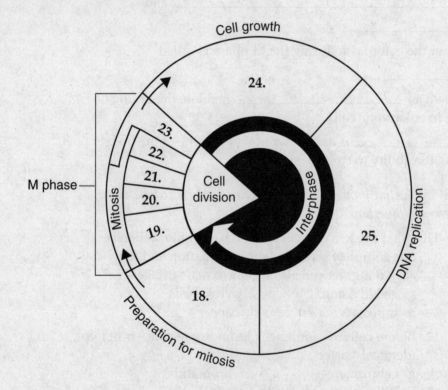

18. _____   22. _____
19. _____   23. _____
20. _____   24. _____
21. _____   25. _____

Prokaryotic and Eukaryotic Cell Division

In order to reproduce, a cell must be able to duplicate its DNA and pass along identical copies to each new daughter cell. This is true for both prokaryotic and eukaryotic cells. However, the two types of cells do not go about DNA replication in the same way. Examination of the differences between prokaryotic and eukaryotic cell cycles gives us an insight into the evolution of more complicated cellular life.

Prokaryotic cells are considered to be simpler than eukaryotic cells because they have only a single, circular molecule of DNA. Prokaryotic cells do not have nuclei, and the DNA molecule is unconfined within the cell membrane. Most prokaryotic cells grow rapidly, and the process of DNA replication occurs throughout most of the cell cycle. There is not enough room in the cell for two complete molecules of DNA. Therefore, when the DNA copy is nearly complete, the replication process stops just long enough for the cell to divide. No visible apparatus, such as the mitotic spindle seen in eukaryotic cells, participates in the division. The two daughter DNA strands are linked to different locations on the plasma membrane to ensure that, during separation, each daughter cell receives an entire copy of the DNA. Unlike mitosis in eukaryotes, there is no condensation or decondensation of DNA.

Eukaryotic cells grow and divide at quite different rates. A yeast cell can divide and double in number in 2 hours; most plant and animal cells take from 10 to 20 hours. The rate at which a cell divides is determined by many factors. However, the chemicals that control the phases of the cell cycle, called growth factors, play an important role. The resting phase of the cell cycle is controlled by the G_0 factor. When the G_1 factor is released, the cell becomes committed to replication. From this point on, a long series of chemical switches turns specific processes on and off. The building of the mitotic spindle and condensation are both under the guidance and timing of these chemical switches. This situation is far more complex than replication in prokaryotic cells, in which replication stops only for the brief moment of cell division. The failure of the chemical switches in eukaryotic cells can cause certain types of cancer.

In the final phases of eukaryotic cell life, the cells are programmed for death. The chromatin in the chromosomes begins to degrade and then the DNA breaks into fragments. The cell eventually digests itself. Programmed cell death is different from cell death resulting from injury or disease. Without it, dead cells would be left to decompose in the body, and other body systems would be required to eliminate the decomposing cell.

Evaluation *Answer the following questions on a separate sheet of paper.*

1. Why are prokaryotic cells considered to be simpler than eukaryotic cells?

2. What prompts a prokaryotic cell to stop replication and undergo cell division?

3. Do eukaryotic cells all divide at the same rate? If not, what controls the rate of division?

4. How is programmed cell death different from cell death as a result of injury or disease?

Chapter 10 Cell Growth and Division   **Graphic Organizer**

Concept Map

Using information from the chapter, complete the concept map below. If there is not enough room in the concept map to write your answers, write them on a separate sheet of paper.

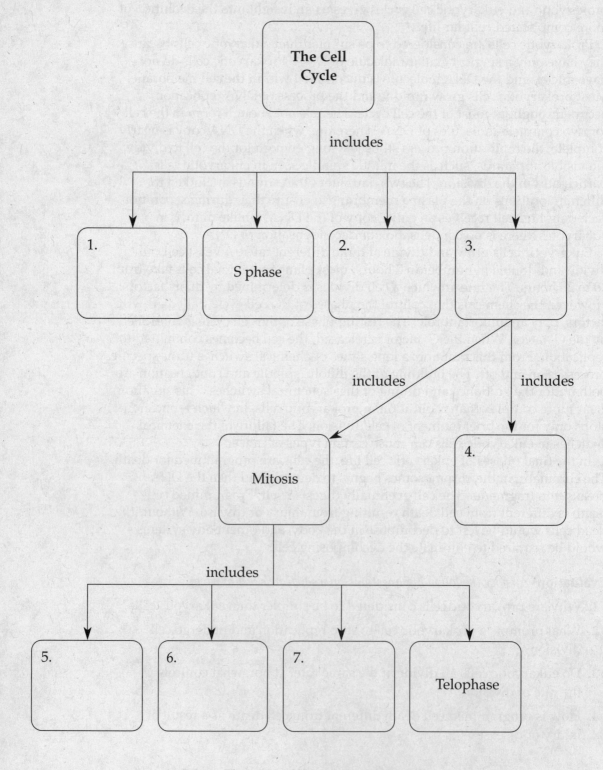

Chapter 10 Cell Growth and Division   **Chapter Test A**

Multiple Choice

Write the letter that best answers the question or completes the statement on the line provided.

_____ 1. As a cell becomes larger, its

   a. volume increases faster than its surface area.

   b. surface area increases faster than its volume.

   c. volume increases, but its surface area stays the same.

   d. surface area stays the same, but its volume increases.

_____ 2. All of the following are problems that growth causes for cells EXCEPT

   a. DNA overload.   c. obtaining enough food.

   b. excess oxygen.   d. expelling wastes.

_____ 3. Which of the following statements is incorrect?

   a. Cell division provides each daughter cell with its own copy of DNA.

   b. Cell division increases the mass of the original cell.

   c. Cell division increases the surface area of the original cell.

   d. Cell division reduces the original cell's volume.

_____ 4. When during the cell cycle are chromosomes visible?

   a. only during interphase

   b. only when they are being replicated

   c. only during the M phase

   d. only during the G_1 phase

_____ 5. Which pair is correct?

   a. G_1 phase, DNA replication

   b. G_2 phase, preparation for mitosis

   c. S phase, cell division

   d. M phase, cell growth

_____ 6. When during the cell cycle is a cell's DNA replicated?

   a. G_1 phase   c. S phase

   b. G_2 phase   d. M phase

_____ 7. Which event occurs during interphase?

   a. The cell grows.   c. Spindle fibers begin to form.

   b. Centrioles appear.   d. Centromeres divide.

_____ 8. During which phase of mitosis do the chromosomes line up along the middle of the dividing cell?

   a. prophase   c. metaphase

   b. telophase   d. anaphase

_____ 9. Which of the following represents the phases of mitosis in their proper sequence?

    a. prophase, metaphase, anaphase, telophase

    b. interphase, prophase, metaphase, anaphase, telophase

    c. interphase, prophase, metaphase, telophase

    d. prophase, metaphase, anaphase, telophase, cytokinesis

_____10. What is the role of the spindle during mitosis?

    a. It helps separate the chromosomes.

    b. It breaks down the nuclear membrane.

    c. It duplicates the DNA.

    d. It divides the cell in half.

_____11. The two main stages of cell division are called

    a. mitosis and interphase.

    b. synthesis and cytokinesis.

    c. the M phase and the S phase.

    d. mitosis and cytokinesis.

_____12. Which of the following is a factor that can stop normal cells from growing?

    a. contact with other cells

    b. growth factors

    c. a cut in the skin

    d. cyclin that has been taken from a cell in mitosis

_____13. Which of the following explains why normal cells grown in a petri dish tend to stop growing once they have covered the bottom of the dish?

    a. The cells lack cyclin.

    b. The petri dish inhibits cell growth.

    c. Contact with other cells stops cell growth.

    d. Most cells grown in petri dishes have a defective p53.

_____14. Cyclins are a family of closely related proteins that

    a. regulate the cell cycle.

    b. produce p53.

    c. cause cancer.

    d. work to heal wounds.

_____15. Cancer is a disorder in which some cells have lost the ability to control their

    a. size.

    b. spindle fibers.

    c. growth rate.

    d. surface area.

Completion

Complete each statement on the line provided.

16. The larger a cell becomes, the _____ efficiently it is able to function.

17. Before a normal cell becomes too large to carry out normal activities, it will usually divide to form two _____ cells.

18. The structure labeled A in Figure 1 is called the _____ .

19. Proteins that regulate the cell cycle based on events inside the cell are called _____ regulators.

20. In all forms of _____ , certain cells fail to respond to the signals that regulate the cell cycle of most cells.

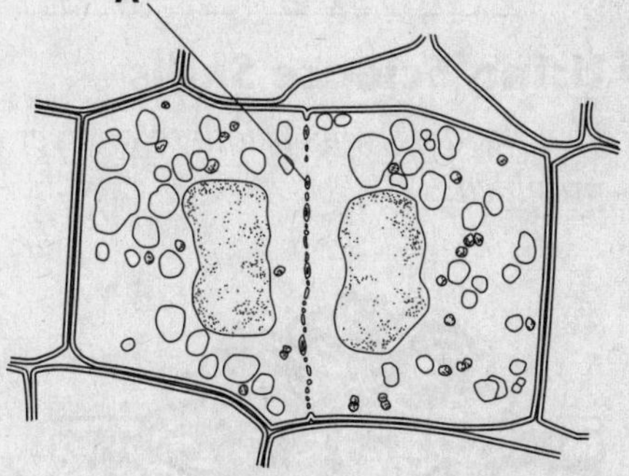

Figure 1

Short Answer

In complete sentences, write the answers to the questions on the lines provided.

21. What effect does cell size have on a cell's ability to efficiently carry out its activities? Give an example.

_____

_____

_____

_____

22. How does an increase in cell size affect the ratio of surface area to volume?

_____

_____

_____

_____

23. What is interphase, and which phases of the cell cycle does interphase include?

_____

_____

_____

_____

24. Describe how a plant cell produces a new cell wall during cytokinesis.

_____

_____

_____

Name________________________ Class________________ Date________

25. Identify a factor that can stop cells from growing. Give an example of how this factor affects cell growth.

Using Science Skills

Use the diagrams below to answer the following questions on the lines provided.

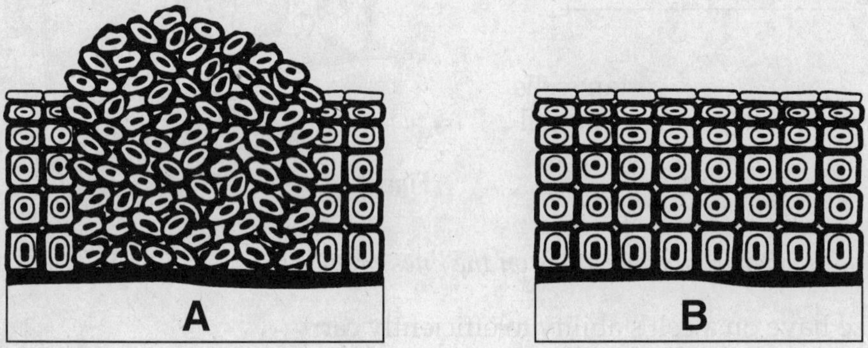

Figure 2

26. **Interpreting Graphics** Look at Figure 2. Which diagram shows cancer cells? How do you know?

27. **Comparing and Contrasting** Explain how cancer cells are different from normal cells. Then, relate these characteristics to the diagrams in Figure 2.

28. **Predicting** Look at the cancer cells shown in Figure 2. What can happen if these cells are left untreated?

29. Applying Concepts Explain the role that p53 might have had in the growth and division of the cells shown in each diagram in Figure 2.

_____

_____

_____

_____

_____

_____

30. Problem Solving How might the cancer cells shown in Figure 2 be prevented from doing more harm to the organism of which they are a part?

_____

_____

_____

_____

_____

Essay

Write the answer to each question in the space provided.

31. What kinds of problems does growth cause for cells? How does cell division help a cell solve these problems?

32. List and describe the main events of the cell cycle. Illustrate your description with a diagram of the cell cycle.

33. Describe what happens during the four phases of mitosis.

34. Describe how the skin cells near a cut behave. What role does contact with other cells have in the behavior of cells near a cut?

35. Describe how cancer cells are different from other cells. Based on these differences, explain why cancer has been such a difficult condition to cure.

Chapter 10 Cell Growth and Division   Chapter Test B

Multiple Choice

Write the letter that best answers the question or completes the statement on the line provided.

____ 1. As a cell grows, it
  a. places more demands on its DNA.
  b. has more trouble moving enough materials across its cell membrane.
  c. both a and b

____ 2. Compared with small cells, large cells have more trouble
  a. dividing.
  b. producing daughter cells.
  c. moving needed materials in and waste products out.

____ 3. The process by which a cell divides into two daughter cells is called
  a. cell division.
  b. metaphase.
  c. interphase.

____ 4. Which of the following happens when a cell divides?
  a. The cell's volume increases.
  b. It becomes more difficult for the cell to get enough oxygen and nutrients.
  c. Each daughter cell receives its own copy of the parent cell's DNA.

____ 5. Which of the following is a phase in the cell cycle?
  a. G_1 phase
  b. M phase
  c. both a and b

____ 6. Cell division is represented in Figure 1 by the letter
  a. A.
  b. D.
  c. C.

____ 7. The cell cycle is the
  a. series of events that cells go through as they grow and divide.
  b. period of time between the birth and the death of a cell.
  c. time from prophase until cytokinesis.

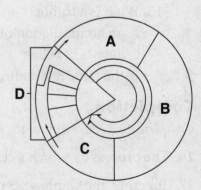

Figure 1

_____ 8. The structure labeled A in Figure 2 is called the
    a. centromere.
    b. centriole.
    c. sister chromatid.

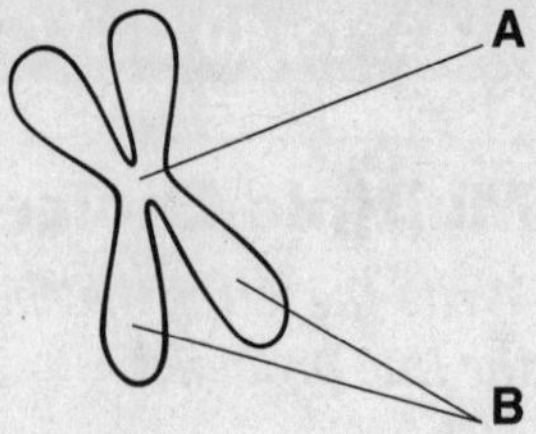

_____ 9. The structures labeled B in Figure 2 are called
    a. centromeres.
    b. centrioles.
    c. sister chromatids.

_____10. Which of the following is a phase of mitosis?
    a. cytokinesis
    b. interphase
    c. anaphase

_____11. The first phase of mitosis is called
    a. prophase.
    b. anaphase.
    c. metaphase.

_____12. In which phase of mitosis do chromosomes become visible?
    a. prophase
    b. interphase
    c. metaphase

_____13. What happens when cells come into contact with other cells?
    a. They divide more quickly.
    b. They stop growing.
    c. They produce cyclins.

_____14. In eukaryotic cells, the timing of the cell cycle is regulated by
    a. the centrioles.
    b. cyclins.
    c. the spindle.

_____15. What is a tumor?
    a. an accumulation of cyclins
    b. a mass of cells
    c. the rapidly dividing cells found at the site of a wound

Figure 2

Completion

Complete each statement on the line provided.

16. The process by which a cell divides into two daughter cells is called _____ .

17. Together, the G_1 phase, S phase, and G_2 phase are called _____ .

18. Another name for cell division is the _____ phase.

19. The process that occurs directly following mitosis is called _____ .

20. Proteins called _____ regulate the timing of the cell cycle in eukaryotic cells.

Short Answer

In complete sentences, write the answers to the questions on the lines provided.

21. List two problems that growth causes for cells.

_____

_____

_____

22. Why are chromosomes not visible in most cells except during cell division?

_____

_____

_____

23. The main events of the cell cycle are labeled A, B, C, and D in Figure 3. Name these events. Then, briefly state what happens during each event.

_____

_____

_____

_____

_____

_____

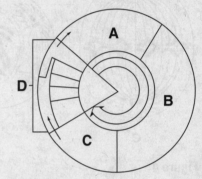

Figure 3

24. Name two factors that help regulate the timing of the cell cycle.

_____

_____

_____

25. How do cancer cells differ from normal cells?

_____

_____

_____

_____

_____

Using Science Skills

Use the diagrams below to answer the following questions on the lines provided.

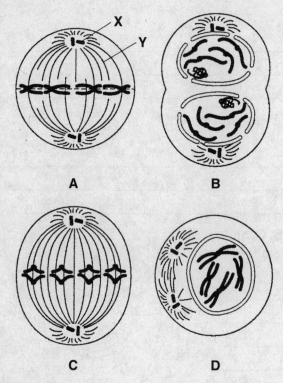

Figure 4

26. **Interpreting Graphics** What does Figure 4 represent? How do you know if this is an animal cell or a plant cell?

   _____

   _____

   _____

27. **Inferring** What is the number of chromosomes in the cell shown in Figure 4?

   _____

28. **Inferring** Identify the structures labeled X and Y in Figure 4.

   _____

29. **Applying Concepts** List the correct order for the diagrams in Figure 4.

   _____

30. **Predicting** After the steps shown in Figure 4 have been arranged in the correct order, what would a diagram of a final step show?

   _____

   _____

Unit 3 Cells   **Unit Test A**

Multiple Choice

Write the letter that best answers the question or completes the statement on the line provided.

____ **1.** In a eukaryote, the portion of the cell outside the nucleus is the
   a. nuclear envelope.
   b. epithelial tissue.
   c. cytoplasm.
   d. organelle.

____ **2.** Which of the following statements is incorrect?
   a. The cell nucleus assembles lipid components of the cell membrane.
   b. The cell nucleus contains nearly all the cell's DNA.
   c. The cell nucleus contains a region where the assembly of ribosomes begins.
   d. The cell nucleus controls many of the cell's activities.

____ **3.** The main function of the cell wall is to
   a. provide a lipid bilayer for the cell membrane.
   b. contain the nucleus outside the cytoplasm.
   c. provide support and protection for the cell.
   d. prevent facilitated diffusion.

____ **4.** A group of similar cells that perform a particular function is called a(an)
   a. organ.
   b. tissue.
   c. organ system.
   d. multicellular organism.

____ **5.** Organisms that use light energy to produce food are called
   a. heterotrophs.
   b. autotrophs.
   c. consumers.
   d. pigments.

____ **6.** Photosynthesis begins when
   a. pigments in photosystem II absorb light.
   b. ATP and NADPH enter the stroma.
   c. pigments in photosytem I absorb light.
   d. high-energy electrons move from photosystem II to photosystem I.

_____ **7.** Which of the following does not affect photosynthesis?
   a. temperature
   b. water availability
   c. light intensity
   d. heterotroph availability

_____ **8.** Which of the following is NOT a stage of cellular respiration?
   a. Krebs cycle
   b. glycolysis
   c. electron transport
   d. fermentation

_____ **9.** The products of lactic acid fermentation are
   a. lactic acid and NAD^+.
   b. pyruvic acid and NADH.
   c. CO_2 and NAD^+.
   d. alcohol and lactic acid.

_____ **10.** In the Krebs cycle, pyruvic acid is
   a. generated so that glycolysis can continue.
   b. broken down into carbon dioxide.
   c. used to convert ATP into ADP.
   d. broken down into glucose.

_____ **11.** In eukaryotes, where is the electron transport chain located?
   a. in the inner membrane of the mitochondrion
   b. in the cytoplasm
   c. in the stroma of the chloroplast
   d. at the center of the mitochondrion

_____ **12.** What is a reactant of cellular respiration?
   a. carbon dioxide
   b. oxygen
   c. fermentation
   d. water

_____ **13.** Which of the following is NOT a problem as a cell becomes larger?
   a. More demands are placed on the cell's DNA.
   b. The cell has more trouble moving nutrients into the cell.
   c. Cell volume decreases as cell surface area increases.
   d. The cell has more trouble moving wastes out of the cell.

_____14. During which phase of the cell cycle are chromosomes
replicated?
   a. M phase
   b. S phase
   c. G_1 phase
   d. G_2 phase

_____15. Cancer cells do not respond to signals that
   a. cause cells to continue to grow.
   b. regulate the growth of most cells.
   c. produce a defect in a gene called p53.
   d. produce contact with other cells.

Completion

Complete each statement on the line provided.

16. The diffusion of water through a selectively permeable membrane
is called _____ .

17. Organisms that obtain energy from the foods they consume are
_____ .

18. The process that uses the energy of sunlight to convert water and
carbon dioxide into high-energy sugars is _____ .

19. In _____, one molecule of glucose is broken in half,
producing two molecules of pyruvic acid.

20. In the process of cell division, the division of the cell nucleus is
called _____ .

Short Answer

*In complete sentences, write the answers to the questions on the lines
provided.*

21. What are the three statements of the cell theory?

_____

_____

_____

22. What is ATP, and how is energy released from it?

_____

_____

_____

_____

23. Write the overall equation for photosynthesis in both symbols and words.

_____

_____

24. Write the overall equation for cellular respiration in both symbols and words.

_____

_____

25. How does cell division affect a cell's ratio of surface area to volume?

_____

_____

_____

Using Science Skills

Use the drawings below to answer the following questions on the lines provided.

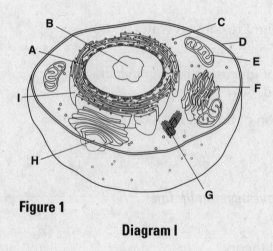

Figure 1

Diagram I

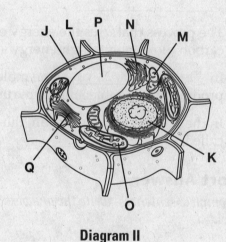

Diagram II

26. Classifying Are the cells in Figure 1 eukaryotes or prokaryotes? Explain how you know.

_____

_____

27. Interpreting Graphics Which cell is an animal cell?

_____

_____

28. Interpreting Graphics Which cell is a plant cell? How do you know?

_____

_____

29. Interpreting Graphics Identify structure O in diagram II. Identify that structure and the process that occurs there.

_____

_____

30. Interpreting Graphics Give the letter of the structure in diagram II of Figure 1 that corresponds to structure E in diagram I. What is that structure, and what process occurs there?

_____

_____

31. Drawing Conclusions From the structures you can identify in the two cells shown in drawings I and II of Figure 1, what do you conclude about the type of cell each drawing depicts?

_____

_____

_____

Essay

Write the answer to each question in the space provided.

32. How are facilitated diffusion and active transport similar, and how do they differ?

33. What happens when pigments obtain energy from light? Use details from the light-dependent reactions in your response.

34. Explain how much energy a cell can produce from a single molecule of glucose when oxygen is available and when oxygen is not available.

35. How are electron carriers essential in both photosynthesis and cellular respiration?

36. What happens during each of the four phases of mitosis in an animal cell?

Multiple Choice

Write the letter that best answers the question or completes the statement on the line provided.

_____ **1.** Which of the following contains a nucleus?

   a. mitochondria

   b. eukaryotes

   c. prokaryotes

_____ **2.** The portion of the cell outside the nucleus is called the

   a. cell wall.

   b. cytoplasm.

   c. cell tissue.

_____ **3.** Which of the following is a function of the cell membrane?

   a. modifies, sorts, and packages proteins

   b. converts sunlight into chemical energy

   c. regulates what enters and leaves the cell

_____ **4.** Cell specialization is a process in which

   a. cells throughout an organism develop in different ways to perform different tasks.

   b. materials move through a cell membrane during exocytosis.

   c. biologists identify different levels of organization.

_____ **5.** One of the principal compounds that cells use to store and release energy is

   a. CO_2.

   b. O_2.

   c. ATP.

_____ **6.** What is the principal pigment of plants?

   a. carbon dioxide

   b. thylakoid

   c. chlorophyll

_____ **7.** The Calvin cycle uses ATP and NADPH to produce

   a. high-energy sugars.

   b. the energy carriers ADP and $NADP^+$.

   c. alcohol and lactic acid.

_____ **8.** The first set of reactions in cellular respiration is
   a. the Krebs cycle.
   b. electron transport.
   c. glycolysis.

_____ **9.** What process releases energy from food molecules by producing ATP in the absence of oxygen?
   a. cellular respiration
   b. photosynthesis
   c. fermentation

_____**10.** The electron transport chain uses high-energy electrons from the Krebs cycle to
   a. break glucose in half.
   b. convert ADP into ATP.
   c. produce high-energy sugars.

_____**11.** Cellular respiration is to mitochondria as photosynthesis is to
   a. osmosis.
   b. microtubules.
   c. chloroplasts.

_____**12.** As a cell grows larger, it has more trouble
   a. replicating its chromosomes.
   b. moving enough nutrients across the cell membrane.
   c. moving through the cell cycle.

_____**13.** The process by which a cell divides into two daughter cells is called
   a. cellular respiration.
   b. cell cyclin.
   c. cell division.

_____**14.** What is cytokinesis?
   a. the division of a cell's cytoplasm
   b. a pigment in the chloroplast
   c. the final phase of interphase

_____**15.** The proteins that regulate the timing of the cell cycle in eukaryotic cells are called
   a. cyclins.
   b. chromatids
   c. tumors.

Completion

Complete each statement on the line provided.

16. The thin, flexible barrier around a cell is called the
    _____.

17. A group of similar cells that perform a particular function is called
    a(an) _____.

18. Plants take in the sun's energy by absorbing _____.

19. Cellular respiration is called an aerobic process because it requires
    _____.

20. Each chromosome consists of two sister _____.

Short Answer

In complete sentences, write the answers to the questions on the lines provided.

21. What does the cell theory state?

    _____

    _____

    _____

22. What is the difference between an autotroph and a heterotroph?

    _____

    _____

    _____

23. In words, write the overall equation for photosynthesis.

    _____

    _____

    _____

24. In words, write the overall equation for cellular respiration.

    _____

    _____

    _____

25. What are the phases of mitosis?

    _____

    _____

    _____

Using Science Skills

Use the drawings below to answer the following questions on the lines provided.

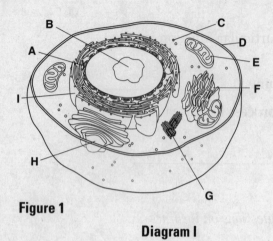

Figure 1

Diagram I

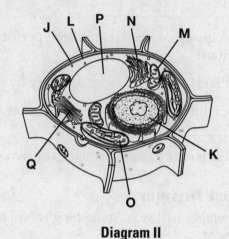

Diagram II

26. Interpreting Graphics Which structure is labeled A in diagram I?

_____

_____

27. Interpreting Graphics Which structure is labeled M in diagram II?

_____

_____

28. Interpreting Graphics Look at diagram II. What is the structure labeled J, and what is its function?

_____

_____

29. Interpreting Graphics In diagram II, what is the structure labeled O?

_____

_____

30. Interpreting Graphics Do the diagrams in Figure 1 represent eukaryotes or prokaryotes? How can you tell?

_____

_____

Chapter 7 Cell Structure and Function

Answers for the Adapted Reading and Study Workbook (worksheets pp. 8–16) can be found in the Adapted Reading and Study Workbook, Annotated Teacher's Edition.

Answers for the Adapted Reading and Study Workbook (worksheets pp. 19–30) can be found in the Adapted Reading and Study Workbook, Annotated Teacher's Edition.

Section Review 7-1

1. living things **2.** structure; function **3.** existing cells **4.** nucleus; prokaryotes **5.** organelles **6.** prokaryotic cell **7.** eukaryotic cell **8.** The giant amoeba is 5000 times larger than the smallest bacterium. **9.** Prokaryotic and eukaryotic cells carry out the functions required for living, and both contain cytoplasm as well as cell membranes. Eukaryotic cells contain organelles and have a nucleus, whereas prokaryotic cells do not. **10.** Eukaryotic; the cells of all multicellular living things, including humans, are eukaryotic.

Section Review 7-2

1. c **2.** a **3.** d **4.** f **5.** g **6.** e **7.** b **8.** Chloroplasts store energy in food molecules. Mitochondria release the energy stored in food molecules. Plants need chloroplasts and mitochondria because they require both functions. **9.** Possible student answer: One function of lysosomes is to remove debris that might clutter a cell. This is analogous to the work a cleanup crew in a factory might perform. **10.** A plant cell has cell walls and chloroplasts, structures not found in animal cells.

Section Review 7-3

1. The cell membrane regulates what enters and leaves the cells and provides protection and support for the cell. **2.** The dissolved molecules will slowly diffuse to the lower concentration side until an equilibrium is established. **3.** Osmosis is the diffusion of water through a selectively permeable membrane. **4.** facilitated diffusion **5.** active transport **6.** hypertonic solution; Water will move out of the cell, causing it to shrink. **7.** isotonic solution; There is equilibrium. Water will move both in and out of the cell, and the cell will not change shape. **8.** hypotonic solution; Water will move into the cell, causing it to swell.

Section Review 7-4

1. Multicellular organisms contain specialized cells so that certain cells can perform particular functions in the organism. **2.** Possible student answers include: Nerve cells: transmit information; Pan-

creatic cells: produce protein enzymes and compounds such as insulin; Red blood cells: transport oxygen; Muscle cells: contract and relax to move body parts. **3.** 2 **4.** 4 **5.** 3 **6.** 1 **7.** A specialized cell in a multicellular organism performs a single life function. A unicellular organism performs all of its necessary life functions. **8.** Possible student answer: The specialized cells of a multicellular organism are analogous to players on a basketball team who possess different skills. The team depends on one player to do most of the dribbling and another player to do most of the rebounding. **9.** The tongue can move and taste, so it must have muscle and nervous tissue. A group of different tissues, like a tongue, is called an organ. **10.** Tissues and organs are different levels of organizations in a multicellular organism. A tissue is a group of similar cells that performs a particular function, whereas an organ consists of groups of tissues that work together.

Chapter Vocabulary Review

1. c **2.** i **3.** f **4.** h **5.** j **6.** e **7.** a **8.** d **9.** b **10.** g **11.** a **12.** c **13.** d **14.** b **15.** c **16.** ribosome **17.** rough endoplasmic reticulum **18.** Golgi apparatus **19.** Mitochondrion **20.** chromosomes **21.** diffusion **22.** lipid bilayer **23.** osmosis **24.** facilitated diffusion **25.** active transport

Enrichment

1. Morphogenesis is the process of cell differentiation, while histogenesis is the development of tissues. These processes are similar because they both involve changes during embryological development and both are required for the development of a multicellular organism. **2.** The instructions for the process of histogenesis are stored in the chromosomes.

Graphic Organizer

1. Plant cells **2.** Chloroplasts **3.** Cell wall **4.** Mitochondria **5.** Ribosomes **6.** Genetic information/DNA

Chapter 7—Test A

Multiple Choice **1.** D **2.** B **3.** C **4.** D **5.** A **6.** C **7.** B **8.** D **9.** D **10.** D **11.** A **12.** A **13.** C **14.** A **15.** C **Completion** **16.** cells **17.** cytoplasm **18.** chromosomes **19.** ribosomes **20.** cell membrane **Short Answer** **21.** Prokaryotes are generally simpler and smaller than eukaryotes, whereas eukaryotes have a nucleus and other specialized organelles. **22.** Structure Q in diagram II corresponds to structure H in diagram I, the Golgi apparatus. The function of the Golgi apparatus is to modify, sort, and package proteins and other materials from the endoplasmic reticulum for storage in the cell or secretion outside the cell. **23.** Structures J and O are found in a plant cell but not in an animal cell. J is the cell wall, which provides support and protection for the cell. O is a chloroplast, an organelle that captures the energy of sunlight and converts it into chemical energy. **24.** Diffusion is a process in which particles tend to move from an area where they are more concentrated to an area where they are less concentrated. **25.** When a blood cell is placed in a hypertonic solution, the water flows from the blood cell, through the cell membrane, into the solution. As a result of losing water, the cell shrinks. **Using Science Skills 26.** The experimental setup shows two solutions with different concentrations of two different solutes separated by a selectively permeable membrane. Over time, the solutes should reach an equilibrium. **27.** Some of the C molecules will move to the B side of the container. **28.** Some of the D molecules will move from side A to side B. The net movement of D molecules will be from side B to side A. **29.** At equilibrium, the concentrations of both C and D molecules will be equal on either side of the selectively permeable membrane. **30.** Yes, both kinds of molecules will continue to move across the membrane; however, there will be no net movement of either molecule. **Essay 31.** The cell theory states that all living things are composed of cells. It also says that cells are the basic units of life and new cells come from preexisting cells. The cell theory is significant to biology because all living thing are made of cells. Differences in the structure and function of different life forms are reflected in differences in their cell structures. **32.** Like a piece of mosaic art, which is made of different pieces, the cell membrane is made of many different molecules. The background is a lipid bilayer. Within this bilayer are proteins that form channels and pumps that help move materials from one side of the membrane to the other. Carbohydrates on the outer surface of the membrane act like chemical identification cards and allow cells to identify one another. **33.** Facilitated diffusion is the movement through a protein channel of molecules that could not otherwise cross the membrane. Facilitated diffusion only occurs with a concentration difference and does not require additional energy. Active transport is the movement of materials across a cell membrane against a concentration difference and does require the addition of energy. **34.** The cell from the unicellular organism carries out all the life processes of the organism. The cell from the multicellular organism is specialized and carries out only certain tasks in the organism, while relying on other cells in the multicellular organism to complete other life processes. **35.** The levels of organization in a multicellular organism include cells, tissues, organs, and organ systems. Similar cells are grouped into tissues; groups of tis-sues that work together form organs; a group of organs that work together make up an organ system.

Chapter 7—Test B

Multiple Choice 1. B **2.** A **3.** C **4.** C **5.** A **6.** C **7.** A **8.** B **9.** C **10.** B **11.** B **12.** B **13.** B **14.** A **15.** C **Completion 16.** cytoplasm **17.** organelles **18.** diffusion **19.** specialization **20.** cells, organs **Short Answer 21.** The cell theory states that all living things are composed of cells, that cells are the basic units of structure and function in living things, and that new cells are produced from existing cells. **22.** The nucleus contains the cell's genetic material in the form of DNA. The nucleus also controls many of the cell's activities. **23.** The cytoskeleton helps the cell maintain its shape. It is also involved in movement. **24.** Because the concentration of water in the cup is greater than the concentration of water in the raisin, water will flow from the cup into the raisin. The water is a hypotonic solution in this example. **25.** cell, tissue, organ, organ system **Using Science Skills 26.** Diagram II, a plant cell, contains such a structure, a chloroplast. **27.** Structure E in diagram I corresponds to structure M in diagram II. This structure is a mitochondrion. **28.** Structure D. **29.** Structure P is a central vacuole. It stores materials such as water, salts, proteins, and carbohydrates. The pressure in the vacuole helps the cell support heavy structures. **30.** Both drawings are of eukaryotes, because each cell has a nucleus.

Chapter 8 Photosynthesis

Answers for the Adapted Reading and Study Workbook (worksheets pp. 54–70) can be found in the Adapted Reading and Study Workbook, Annotated Teacher's Edition.

Answers for the Adapted Reading and Study Workbook (worksheets pp. 63–70) can be found in the Adapted Reading and Study Workbook, Annotated Teacher's Edition.

Section Review 8-1

1. Autotrophs get energy from the sun in the form of light energy. **2.** ATP is used to store energy needed for life processes. **3.** ADP is converted to ATP by the addition of another phosphate group to an ADP molecule. **4.** When ATP is changed to ADP, a phosphate group is removed. The removal of a phosphate group releases energy to the cell. **5.** The energy stored in ATP is used for active transport and for movement within cells. **6.** They are similar in that they both depend on energy from food. However, autotrophs use the sun's energy to make their own food, while the heterotrophs obtain their energy from the foods they eat. Heterotrophs eat autotrophs or other heterotrophs. **7.** heterotroph **8.** autotroph **9.** heterotroph

Section Review 8-2

1. c **2.** b **3.** a **4.** b **5.** c **6.** $6CO_2 + 6H_2O \overset{light}{\Rightarrow} C_6H_{12}O_6$ + $6O_2$ or carbon dioxide + water $\overset{light}{\Rightarrow}$ sugars + oxygen **7.** Light energy is transferred to the electrons in the chlorophyll molecule, raising the energy of these electrons. These high-energy electrons make photosynthesis work. **8.** The production of food will drop because plants do not absorb light well in the green region of the visible spectrum. **9.** The plant would have leaves of an orange color. The orange pigment carotene absorbs the orange wavelength of light very poorly, which makes the leaves appear orange. **10.** Students' experiments should have controls and manipulated and responding variables, and should test an effect of air pollution on photosynthesis. For example, two plants are placed in different atmospheres, one containing few pollutants and the other containing many pollutants. The students would observe the plants and record data on how the plants thrive or survive in different atmospheres.

Section Review 8-3

1. thylakoid **2.** Calvin cycle **3.** ATP, NADPH **4.** oxygen **5.** light-independent **6.** stroma **7.** Both systems are light dependent. Both systems use light energy to energize electrons. One difference is that water molecules are split in photosystem II, but not in photosystem I. In photosystem II, ADP is converted into ATP. **8.** The Calvin cycle is a light-independent reaction and does not require light. It will continue as long as there are ATP and NADPH molecules for the cycle to use. **9.** The rate of photosynthesis is affected by water, temperature, and light. Low amounts of water, low temperatures, very high temperatures, and little light will slow the rate, while adequate amounts of water, moderate temperatures, and sunny weather will increase the rate. **10.** Students should indicate that they would measure either oxygen or carbon dioxide, and that the rate of increase in oxygen or decrease in carbon dioxide would indicate the rate of photosynthesis.

Chapter Vocabulary Review

1. Adenosine triphosphate is one of the principal chemical compounds that living things use to store energy. **2.** A thylakoid is a saclike, photosynthetic membrane found in chloroplasts that contains clusters of chlorophyll. **3.** $NADP^+$ stands for nicotinamide adenine dinucleotide phosphate, a carrier molecule, which accepts and holds 2 high-energy electrons along with a hydrogen ion. **4.** ATP synthase is a protein found in the thylakoid membrane and allows H^+ ions to pass through it. ATP synthase binds ADP and a phosphate group together to produce ATP. **5.** The Calvin cycle uses ATP and NADPH from the light-dependent reactions to produce high-energy sugars. The Calvin cycle takes

place in the stroma of chloroplasts and does not require light. **6.** An autotroph is an organism that makes its own food. A heterotroph is an organism that obtains energy from the food it consumes. **7.** Oxygen is produced in the light-dependent reactions of photosynthesis. **8.** Pigments are light-absorbing molecules. Chlorophyll is a pigment. **9.** The light-dependent reaction uses energy from sunlight to produce ATP, NADPH, and oxygen. The Calvin cycle does not depend on light and uses ATP and NADPH to produce high-energy sugars. **10.** Sugars are formed from carbon dioxide in the Calvin cycle. **11.** c **12.** e **13.** b **14.** a **15.** d **16.** light **17.** H_2O **18.** CO_2 **19.** O_2 **20.** sugars

Enrichment

1. Radio waves have the longest wavelength on the electromagnetic spectrum. Gamma rays have the shortest wavelength. **2.** Bees can see the beginning of the ultraviolet section of the electromagnetic spectrum where the frequencies are close to those of visible light.

Graphic Organizer

1. H_2O **2.–3.** NADPH, ATP **4.** CO_2 **5.–6.** $NADP^+$, ADP + P

Chapter 8—Test A

Multiple Choice 1. D **2.** C **3.** D **4.** D **5.** C **6.** B **7.** D **8.** A **9.** B **10.** B **11.** D **12.** B **13.** A **14.** B **15.** C **Completion 16.** chlorophyll **17.** green **18.** green **19.** B **20.** decreases **Short Answer** **21.** Heterotrophs obtain energy from the food they consume. **22.** ATP, or adenosine triphosphate, is one of the principal compounds that cells use to store and release energy. Energy is released from ATP when the chemical bond between the second and third phosphates is broken and the third phosphate group is released.

23.
$$6CO_2 + 6H_2O \overset{light}{\to} C_6H_{12}O_6 + 6O_2$$

carbon dioxide + water $\overset{light}{\to}$ sugar + oxygen

24. Sample answer: By being close together, electrons and energy can easily move through the photosystems powering each successive step of the light-dependent reactions. **25.** The Calvin cycle uses ATP and NADPH from the light-dependent reactions to produce high-energy sugars. **Using Science Skills** **26.** The beaker she placed in the shade is the control. **27.** The air bubbles are probably oxygen gas. Jan Ingenhousz showed that plants produce oxygen bubbles in the light but not in the dark. **28.** 5 cm **29.** The student's data show that as the light gets farther from the water plant, the water plant gives off less bubbles. **30.** Probably not; light intensity increases the rate of photosynthesis up to a certain point and then levels off. **Essay** **31.** Heterotrophs depend on autotrophs to obtain energy from the sun. This energy is then passed on to heterotrophs in the form of food. Without autotrophs, the sun's energy would not be available to heterotrophs and heterotrophs would eventually die out or find a new way of obtaining energy. **32.** A glucose molecule can store more than 90 times the chemical energy than an ATP molecule. Glucose is used by cells to store large amounts of energy for long periods of time. In contrast, ATP is used to store smaller amounts of energy that will be used in the next few seconds. Cells can regenerate ATP from ADP as needed by using the energy in foods like glucose. **33.** Light is a form of energy; thus, when a pigment absorbs light it also absorbs the energy from that light. When the pigment chlorophyll absorbs light, much of the energy is transferred directly to electrons in the chlorophyll molecule, raising the energy levels of these electrons. This energy is then passed on in the reactions of photosynthesis. **34.** Three of the factors that affect the rate of photosynthesis are light intensity, temperature, and water. The rate of photosynthesis increases with light intensity up to a certain point, then levels off. Photosynthesis slows at extreme temperatures and usually has an optimal temperature for each kind of plant. Lack of water slows down photosynthesis. **35.** Electrons in the pigments in photosystem II absorb energy from light. These electrons then move through the electron transport chain to photosystem I. H^+ ions move from the stroma into the inner thylakoid membrane. $NADP^+$ becomes NADPH. The charge difference on either side of the thylakoid membrane provides the energy to make ATP via ATP synthase.

Chapter 8—Test B

Multiple Choice **1.** A **2.** B **3.** C **4.** C **5.** A **6.** C **7.** B **8.** A **9.** A **10.** A **11.** C **12.** B **13.** A **14.** C **15.** C **Completion** **16.** heterotrophs **17.** light **18.** high-energy sugars **19.** the stroma **20.** ATP **Short Answer** **21.** Autotrophs are organisms, such as plants, that can make their own food. Heterotrophs, such as animals, must use food made by other organisms to get energy. **22.** Heterotrophs get energy by eating autotrophs and/or other heterotrophs. **23.** When a phosphate group is removed from ATP, energy is released and ADP results. **24.** The structures are thylakoids. They contain photosystems that are able to capture the energy of sunlight. **25.** Any two of the following: water, light intensity, temperature **Using Science Skills** **26.** photosynthesis **27.** a chloroplast **28.** Oxygen gas, ATP, and NADPH are the products of the light-dependent reactions. **29.** sugars **30.** CO_2

Chapter 9 Cellular Respiration

Answers for the Adapted Reading and Study Workbook (worksheets pp. 92–98) can be found in the Adapted Reading and Study Workbook, Annotated Teacher's Edition.

Answers for the Adapted Reading and Study Workbook (worksheets pp. 101–108) can be found in the Adapted Reading and Study Workbook, Annotated Teacher's Edition.

Section Review 9-1

1. cellular respiration **2.** glucose **3.** NADH **4.** two **5.** alcohol, CO_2, NAD^+ **6.** The process of fermentation does not require oxygen. **7.** Fermentation continues to produce NAD^+ without oxygen. This process allows glycolysis to continue to produce ATP. **8.** glucose **9.** 2 NADH **10.** 2 molecules of pyruvic acid

Section Review 9-2

1. Pyruvic acid is the product of glycolysis and becomes one of the reactants in the Krebs cycle. It is broken down into carbon dioxide to produce ATP. **2.** Glycolysis is the first step in cellular respiration. The pyruvic acid produced during glycolysis is broken down in the presence of oxygen during the Krebs cycle. **3.** High-energy electrons from the Krebs cycle and glycolysis are used to convert ADP to ATP in the electron transport chain. **4.** The reactants in cellular respiration are glucose and oxygen. The products of cellular respiration are carbon dioxide, water, and energy. **5.** photosynthesis **6.** photosynthesis **7.** cellular respiration **8.** cellular respiration **9.** Only 2 ATP are obtained from glycolysis, while a total of 36 ATP are obtained from cellular respiration. **10.** The baseball player would probably use lactic acid fermentation, and the cross-country skier would use cellular respiration. The baseball player would need quick energy and an ATP supply for only a few seconds. The cross-country skier would need to generate a continuing supply of ATP for a longer period of time.

Chapter Vocabulary Review

1. A calorie is the amount of energy needed to raise the temperature of 1 gram of water 1 Celsius degree. **2.** Glycolysis is the process in which one molecule of glucose is broken in half, producing two molecules of pyruvic acid, a 3-carbon compound. **3.** Cellular respiration is the process that releases energy by breaking down glucose and other food molecules in the presence of oxygen. **4.** NAD^+ is an electron carrier that helps pass energy from glucose to other pathways in the cell during glycolysis. **5.** Fermentation is the process that releases energy from food molecules by producing ATP in the absence of oxygen. **6.** Anaerobic means "not in air." **7.** Aerobic means "in air." **8.** The Krebs cycle is the process in which pyruvic acid is broken down into carbon dioxide in a series of energy-extracting reactions. **9.** The electron transport chain uses the high-energy electrons from the Krebs cycle to convert ADP to ATP. **10.** alcoholic fermentation **11.** lactic acid fermentation **12.** cellular respiration **13.** glycolysis **14.** cellular respiration **15.** lactic acid fermentation **16.** b **17.** d **18.** c **19.** glycolysis **20.** Krebs cycle

Enrichment

1. Student responses should suggest that adding the cup of yogurt to the unfermented milk would introduce *Lactobacillus* bacteria to the bowl of fresh milk, allowing it to ferment also. This is, in fact, exactly how fermented milk products are made. Active cultures of *Lactobacilli* are added to the products to ferment them. **2.** Lactic acid slows the growth of bacteria and other organisms that cause food to spoil.

Graphic Organizer

1. Quick production of ATP and NADH for cellular energy **2.** Release of energy without oxygen **3.** Long-term, slow production of ATP for cellular energy **4.** Glucose, ATP **5.** Pyruvic acid, NADH **6.** ATP, NADH, pyruvic acid **7.** CO_2, H_2O, energy **8.** Can release energy without oxygen **9.** Sustains energy production much longer than glycolysis and fermentation **10.** Quickly fills all available NAD^+ molecules with electrons and the process stops **11.** Much slower than glycolysis and fermentation

Chapter 9—Test A

Multiple Choice **1.** A **2.** C **3.** D **4.** C **5.** C **6.** D **7.** C **8.** C **9.** A **10.** C **11.** B **12.** B **13.** B **14.** C **15.** B **Completion** **16.** oxygen **17.** 2 **18.** alcoholic **19.** C **20.** lactic acid **Short Answer** **21.** The three stages are as follows: glycolysis (which occurs in the cytoplasm), the Krebs cycle (which occurs in the mitochondria), and electron transport (which occurs in the mitochondria). **22.** Alcoholic fermentation produces carbon dioxide, alcohol, and NAD^+; lactic acid fermentation produces lactic acid and NAD^+. **23.** Sample answer: Lactic acid fermentation does not give off carbon dioxide as shown by pathway A in the figure. **24.** Oxygen is the final electron acceptor in the electron transport chain, which means that it is needed to get rid of low-energy electrons and H^+ ions. **25.** The body uses ATP that is already present in the muscle cells, ATP made from lactic acid fermentation, and ATP made from cellular respiration. **Using Science Skills** **26.** Sample answer: The equation for cellular respiration is $6O_2 + C_6H_{12}O_6 \rightarrow 6CO_2 + 6H_2O + $ Energy. The mouse should give off CO_2.

27. Sample answer: The mouse requires oxygen. Fresh air containing oxygen flows from outside the flasks into flasks B, C, and D. Air mixed with whatever the mouse gives off flows from flask B into flask A. The mouse receives fresh air and should be able to survive in the chamber for the duration of the experiment. **28.** Sample answer: If the mouse is carrying out cellular respiration, it will give off CO_2, the CO_2 will flow into flask A, and the phenolphthalein in flask A will change from pink to clear. **29.** Sample answer: The cricket, like all living organisms, is carrying out cellular respiration. However, the mouse is larger than the cricket and will give off more CO_2 than the cricket. After one hour, the cricket probably has not given off enough CO_2 to measure. If the scientist allows the experiment to continue for several hours, she will see that more CO_2 is given off by the cricket over time. **30.** Sample answer: The mouse that had been exercising should give off more CO_2 because this mouse will be breathing more heavily. This mouse might even have an oxygen debt to repay. **Essay** **31.** Sample answer: Glycolysis is the breakdown of glucose into two molecules of pyruvic acid, producing 4 ATP molecules. An initial input of 2 ATP molecules is required to start glycolysis; thus, there is a net gain of 2 ATP molecules. This process produces high-energy electrons, which are passed to NAD^+ forming 2 NADH. If oxygen is present, glycolysis leads to the Krebs cycle and the electron transport chain. If oxygen is not present, glycolysis is followed by the rest of fermentation. **32.** Both main types of fermentation release energy from food molecules by producing ATP in the absence of oxygen. Alcoholic fermentation occurs in yeasts and a few other microorganisms, and its products are alcohol, CO_2, and NAD^+. Lactic acid fermentation occurs in muscle cells and some unicellular organisms, and its products are lactic acid and NAD^+.
33. Sample answer: The electron carriers of cellular respiration are NAD^+ and FAD. These molecules accept high-energy electrons and move to the electron transport chain. The electron transport chain produces ATP molecules. **34.** The electron transport chain uses the high-energy electrons from the Krebs cycle to convert ADP into ATP. High-energy electrons are passed from one carrier protein to the next. Every 2 high-energy electrons that move down the chain result in enough energy to convert 3 ADP molecules to 3 ATP molecules, on average. **35.** Sample answer: The first few seconds of a race, for example, are powered by the ATP that the muscle cells already have on hand. Then, the muscle cells begin producing ATP by lactic acid fermentation. After about 90 seconds, however, cellular respiration is the only way to generate a continuing supply of ATP.

Chapter 9—Test B

Multiple Choice **1.** C **2.** A **3.** B **4.** A **5.** A **6.** C **7.** C **8.** C **9.** C **10.** C **11.** A **12.** B **13.** C **14.** C **15.** B **Completion** **16.** pyruvic acid **17.** electron transport chain **18.** oxygen **19.** 2 **20.** 36 **Short Answer** **21.** Cellular respiration is the process that releases energy by breaking down food molecules in the presence of oxygen. **22.** During glycolysis, one molecule of glucose is broken in half, producing two molecules of pyruvic acid. **23.** Citric acid is the first compound formed in the process. **24.** The electron transport chain uses high-energy electrons from the Krebs cycle to convert ADP into ATP. **25.** Photosynthesis releases oxygen into the atmosphere, whereas cellular respiration uses oxygen to release energy from food. **Using Science Skills** **26.** The figure shows the electron transport chain. **27.** The electrons come from NADH and FADH$_2$, electron carriers that come from the Krebs cycle. **28.** They join with 4 H$^+$ and O$_2$ to form water molecules. **29.** The H$^+$ ions are mostly moving into the intermembrane space. This movement causes the intermembrane space to become positively charged. **30.** Sample answer: ATP synthase catalyzes the reaction that produces ATP from ADP and a phosphate.

Chapter 10 Cell Growth and Division

Answers for the Adapted Reading and Study Workbook (worksheets pp. 130–135) can be found in the Adapted Reading and Study Workbook, Annotated Teacher's Edition.

Answers for the Adapted Reading and Study Workbook (worksheets pp. 138–143) can be found in the Adapted Reading and Study Workbook, Annotated Teacher's Edition.

Section Review 10-1

1. cell membrane **2.** surface area **3.** cell division **4.** The information contained in the DNA would not be able to meet the needs of the larger cell. **5.** Food, oxygen, and water enter the cell, and waste products exit the cell via the cell membrane. **6.** The ratio of surface area to volume decreases as the cell's size increases. **7.** Cells divide because of the problems of DNA "overload" and of increasing size that decreases the ratio of surface area to volume. **8.** 6 cm^3 **9.** 6:1 **10.** 80 cm^2

Section Review 10-2

1. The four phases of the cell cycle are the M phase (mitosis), G$_1$ phase (cell growth), S phase (DNA replication), and G$_2$ phase. **2.** The cell replicates its chromosomes. **3.** During cytokinesis, the cytoplasm divides from one cell into two cells. **4.** metaphase **5.** prophase **6.** prophase **7.** anaphase **8.** telophase **9.** prophase **10.** metaphase **11.** anaphase **12.** Mitosis refers only to the division of the nucleus, while cell division also includes cytokinesis, or division of the cytoplasm. **13.** There would be 64 cells after 7.5 hours. **14.** Possible student answers may include any reference to incorrect movement of chromosomes during mitosis, lack of cytokinesis, or DNA duplication without cell division. **15.** An animal cell has centrioles, while a plant cell has regions known as centromeres. During cytokinesis, in most animal cells the cell membrane moves inward and pinches the cytoplasm into two equal parts. In a plant cell, a cell plate forms midway between the two divided nuclei.

Section Review 10-3

1. Cyclin regulates the timing of the cell cycle in eukaryotic cells. **2.** Internal regulators prevent a cell from entering mitosis until all chromosomes have been replicated. **3.** External regulators, such as growth factors, direct cells to speed up or slow down the cell cycle. **4.** The abnormal growth of cancer cells is caused by the failure to respond to signals that regulate growth. **5.** No. Some cells complete the cell cycle more quickly than other cells, or spend more time in one phase than another. External regulators can also alter the growth rate. For example, when there is an injury to the skin, the cells will increase their growth rate. Another example is when molecules on the surface of neighboring cells cause a cell to decrease its growth rate. **6.** Possible student answer: How much cyclin is in cancer cells? **7.** Both internal and external regulators regulate the timing of the cell cycle. The external regulators respond to stimuli from outside the cell, and the internal regulators respond to stimuli within the cell. **8.** Possible student answer: A cut or injury is followed by a period of increased cell growth. After healing is complete, the cells return to a normal rate of growth.

Chapter Vocabulary Review

1. cell division **2.** centromere **3.** interphase **4.** cell cycle **5.** spindle **6.** Mitosis **7.** prophase, metaphase, anaphase, telophase **8.** cytokinesis **9.** cyclins **10.** cancer **11.** a **12.** c **13.** b **14.** a **15.** a **16.** b **17.** d **18.** G$_2$ phase **19.** prophase **20.** metaphase **21.** anaphase **22.** telophase **23.** cytokinesis **24.** G$_1$ phase **25.** S phase

Enrichment

1. Prokaryotes have a single circular molecule of DNA and no nucleus. The DNA molecule is unconfined within the cell membrane. **2.** When a prokaryote has completely replicated its entire strand of DNA, the resulting double molecule is too big for the cell to hold. The cell divides to make room for both molecules, halting the process of replication just long enough to do this. **3.** Eukaryotes divide at very different rates. Yeast can divide as quickly as every 2 hours; some plants and animal cells take up to 10 to 20 hours. The rate of division is controlled by chemicals called growth factors. **4.** In programmed cell death, the dying cell digests itself. Cell death due to injury or disease is premature and does not follow the same pattern.

Graphic Organizer

1. G_1 phase **2.** G_2 phase **3.** M phase **4.** Cytokinesis **5.** Prophase **6.** Metaphase **7.** Anaphase

Chapter 10—Test A

Multiple Choice **1.** A **2.** B **3.** B **4.** C **5.** B **6.** C **7.** A **8.** C **9.** A **10.** A **11.** D **12.** A **13.** C **14.** A **15.** C **Completion** **16.** less **17.** daughter **18.** cell plate **19.** internal **20.** cancer **Short Answer** **21.** A large cell carries out its activities less efficiently than a small cell does. For example, as a cell's size increases, it becomes more difficult for needed materials, such as oxygen and nutrients, to reach all the parts of the cell. **22.** As the size of a cell increases, its ratio of surface area to volume decreases. **23.** Interphase is the period of cell growth in between cell divisions. Interphase includes the G_1 phase, the S phase, and the G_2 phase. **24.** During cytokinesis, a cell plate forms in the cytoplasm midway between each new nucleus. The cell plate gradually develops into a separating membrane, and a cell wall begins to appear in the cell plate. **25.** Contact with other cells can stop cell growth. **Using Science Skills** **26.** Diagram A shows cancer cells because it shows cells that are not growing in an organized way. **27.** Cancer cells do not respond to the signals that regulate growth in most cells. Diagram B shows cells that are normal and have responded to such signals. Diagram A shows cells that have divided until they have formed a mass of cells, or a tumor. The cancer cells are dividing uncontrollably and are disrupting nearby normal cells. **28.** They can break loose from the tumor they are now a part of and spread throughout the body, disrupting normal activities and causing serious medical problems. **29.** Diagram A—these cells might have a defect in the p53 gene, which has allowed the cells to multiply more quickly than the normal cells. Diagram B—these cells probably have a healthy copy of the p53 gene, which has stopped the cell cycle until the genetic material in these cells has been properly copied. **30.** Students may suggest removing the cancerous cells in hopes of preventing their continued division, growth, and spread throughout the body, or treating them with

radiation or chemicals that will destroy the cells. **Essay** **31.** As a cell grows, it functions less efficiently because it places more demands on its DNA and it is less able to move materials to their proper destinations quickly. Cell division results in two daughter cells. Each cell has its own copy of the parent cell's DNA and has a size that allows it to efficiently exchange materials. **32.** During the G_1 phase, the cell grows; during the S phase, the DNA replicates; during the G_2 phase, the cell prepares for mitosis. The M phase or cell division includes mitosis and cytokinesis. Figures should approximate Figure 10-4 on page 245 of the student text. **33.** Prophase—the chromatin condenses into chromosomes, the centrioles separate (in animal cells), and the nuclear envelope breaks down; Metaphase—the chromosomes line up across the midline of the cell and each chromosome is attached to a spindle fiber and centromere; Anaphase—sister chromatids separate into individual chromsomes; Telophase—chromosomes move to opposite sides of the dividing cell and two new nuclear envelopes form. **34.** Cells at the edges of the cut are stimulated to divide rapidly, producing new cells, and healing the wound. When the cut is almost completely healed, the rate of cell division slows down. Thus, when the cells on either side of the cut are no longer in contact with one another, they divide to fill in the gap. Once the cells are in contact with one another (the cut is healed), the cells resume their normal growth rate. **35.** Sample answer: Unlike normal cells, cancer cells do not respond to normal controls on growth and division. By dividing uncontrollably, cancer cells form tumors and spread throughout the body. A cure for cancer includes a way to both prevent cancer cells from dividing uncontrollably and to allow normal cells to continue dividing normally. Finding a way to stop the cell cycle in some cells, but not interfere with the cell cycle in other cells, has made it difficult to cure cancer.

Chapter 10—Test B

Multiple Choice **1.** C **2.** C **3.** A **4.** C **5.** C **6.** B **7.** A **8.** A **9.** C **10.** C **11.** A **12.** A **13.** B **14.** B **15.** B **Completion** **16.** cell division **17.** interphase **18.** M **19.** cytokinesis **20.** cyclins **Short Answer** **21.** As a cell grows larger, more demands are placed on its DNA and the cell has more trouble moving enough nutrients and wastes across the cell membrane. **22.** Chromosomes aren't visible because the DNA and protein molecules that make up the chromosomes are spread throughout the nucleus. **23.** A—G_1 phase, cell growth; B—S phase, DNA replication; C—G_2 phase, preparation for mitosis; D—M phase, cell division (mitosis and cytokinesis) **24.** Any two of the following: contact with other cells, cyclins, growth factors, and any other internal or external regulators **25.** Cancer cells do not respond to the signals that control the growth of normal cells. As a result, cancer cells form tumors and can spread throughout the body. **Using Science Skills 26.** It shows various stages of mitosis in an animal cell. This is an animal cell because of the presence of centrioles. **27.** Four **28.** X is the centriole; Y is the spindle. **29.** D, A, C, B **30.** The final step would be cytokinesis. It would show two daughter cells forming.

Unit 3—Test A

Multiple Choice 1. C **2.** A **3.** C **4.** B **5.** B **6.** A **7.** D **8.** D **9.** A **10.** B **11.** A **12.** B **13.** C **14.** D **15.** B
Completion 16. osmosis **17.** heterotrophs **18.** photosynthesis **19.** glycolysis **20.** mitosis
Short Answer 21. All living things are composed of cells. Cells are the basic units of structure and function in living things. New cells are produced from existing cells. **22.** ATP, or adenosine triphosphate, is one of the principal compounds that cells use to store and release energy. Energy is released when the chemical bond between the second and third phosphates is broken.

23. $6CO_2 + 6\,H_2O \xrightarrow{\text{light}} C_6H_{12}O_6 + 6O_2$

carbon dioxide + water $\xrightarrow{\text{light}}$ sugars + oxygen

24. $6O_2 + C_6H_{12}O_6 \rightarrow 6CO_2 + 6\,H_2O + \text{energy}$

oxygen + glucose $\rightarrow$ carbon dioxide + water + energy

25. Cell division causes the ratio of surface area to volume to become greater in the daughter cells.
Using Science Skills 26. Both drawings are of eukaryotes because each cell has a nucleus.
27. Diagram I. **28.** Diagram II is a plant cell. You can tell it is a plant cell because it contains a nucleus, a chloroplast, and a central vacuole. **29.** Structure D is a chloroplast, where photosynthesis occurs.
30. Structure M corresponds to structure E. Both are mitochondria, where cellular respiration occurs.
Essay 31. They are similar in that both involve the movement of materials across a membrane. Facilitated diffusion involves movement of particles across the membrane through protein channels. Yet, this process does not require use of the cell's energy because it is still diffusion. Active transport, by contrast, does require use of the cell's energy because it is the movement of materials against a concentration difference. **32.** When pigments in photosystem II absorb light, the light energy is absorbed by elec-

trons, increasing their energy level. These high-energy electrons are used in the light-dependent reactions to convert ADP and $NADP^+$ into the energy carriers ATP and NADPH. They provide the energy to build high-energy sugars in the Calvin cycle.
33. The process of releasing energy from glucose is begun with glycolysis, which yields 2 molecules of ATP. When oxygen is not available, glycolysis is followed by fermentation, which produces no more ATP molecules. When oxygen is available, cellular respiration can occur. That pathway results in the production of 34 more ATP molecules, for a total of 36 ATP molecules from a single molecule of glucose.
34. In the process of photosynthesis, the light-dependent reactions convert the electron carrier $NADP^+$ into NADPH, which provides energy to build high-energy sugars in the Calvin cycle. In cellular respiration, the electron carriers $NADP^+$ and FAD^+ are used to make NADPH and $FADH_2$. The electrons in those compounds are used in the electron transport chain to convert ADP to ATP. **35.** During prophase, the chromatin condenses into chromosomes. The centrioles separate, and a spindle begins to form. The nuclear envelope breaks down. During metaphase, the chromosomes line up across the center of the cell. Each chromosome is connected to a spindle fiber at its centromere. During anaphase, the sister chromosomes separate into individual chromosomes and are moved apart. During telophase, the chromosomes gather at opposite ends of the cell and lose their distinct shapes. Two new nuclear envelopes form.

Unit 3—Test B

Multiple Choice 1. B **2.** B **3.** C **4.** A **5.** C **6.** C **7.** A **8.** C **9.** C **10.** B **11.** C **12.** B **13.** C **14.** A **15.** A **Completion 16.** cell membrane **17.** tissue **18.** sunlight **19.** oxygen **20.** chromatids **Short Answer 21.** All living things are composed of cells. Cells are the basic units of structure and function in living things. New cells are produced from existing cells. **22.** An autotroph makes its own food, whereas a heterotroph obtains energy from the foods it eats. **23.** carbon dioxide + water $\xrightarrow{\text{light}}$ sugars + oxygen **24.** oxygen + glucose $\rightarrow$ carbon dioxide + water + energy **25.** Prophase, metaphase, anaphase, telophase **Using Science Skills 26.** Structure A is a cell nucleus. **27.** Structure M is a mitochondrion. **28.** Structure J is a cell wall. Its function is to provide support and protection for the cell. **29.** Structure O is a chloroplast. **30.** They represent eukaryotic cells, because each of the two cells has a nucleus.

Flowchart

Topic:

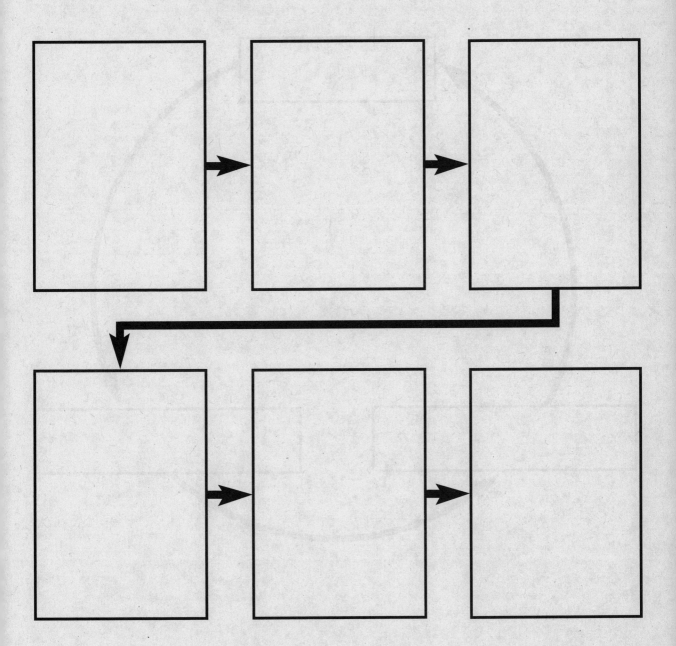

Cycle Diagram

Topic:

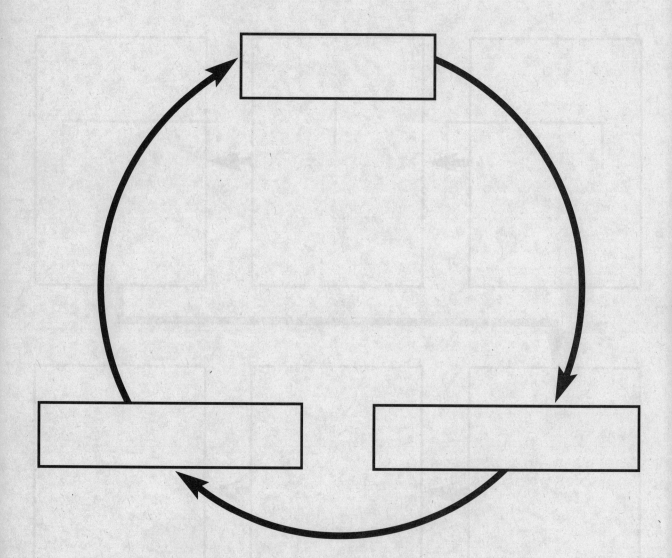

Concept Circle

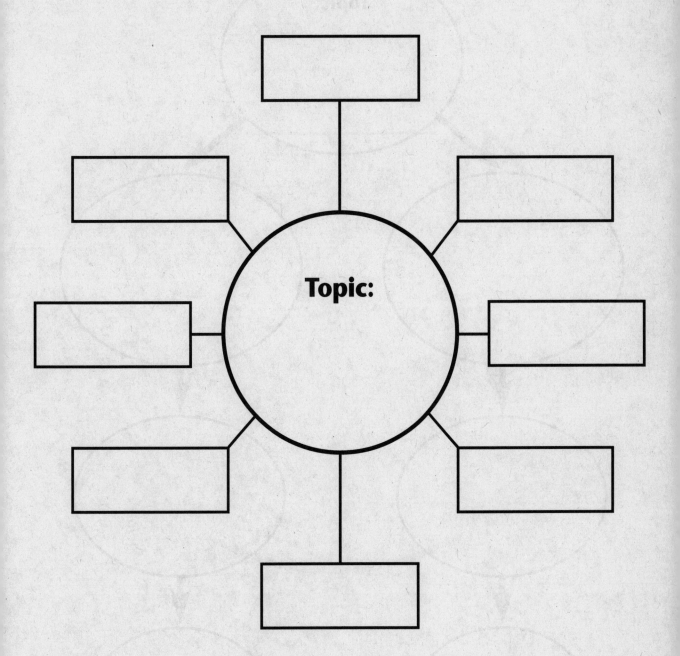

Topic:

Modified Concept Map

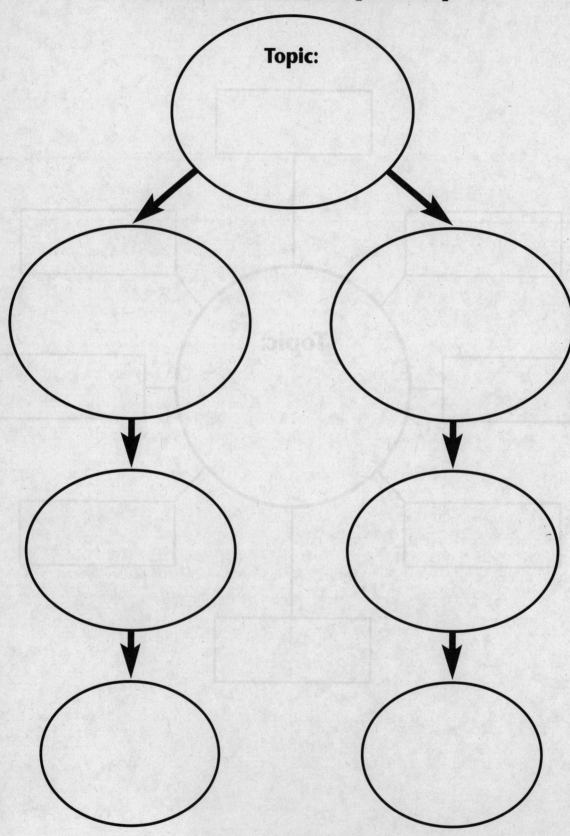

Topic:

Cause/Effect Chart

Topic: _____

Cause	Effect

Compare/Contrast Chart

Topic:

Similarities	Differences

Venn Diagram

Topic: _____   **Topic:** _____

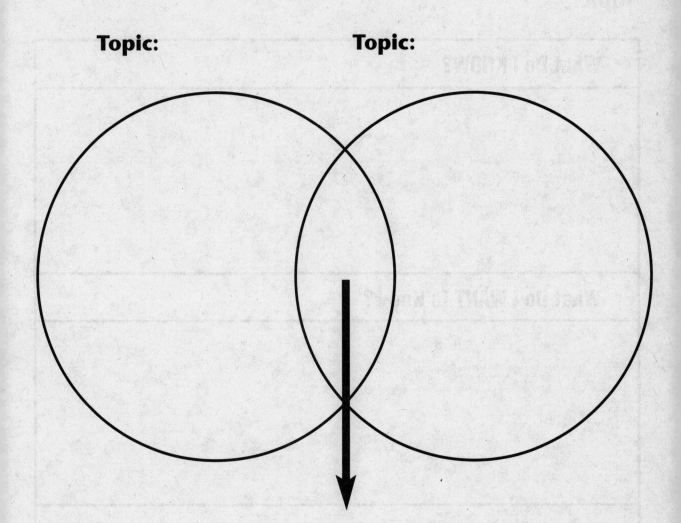

KWL Chart

Topic:

What Do I KNOW?
What Do I WANT to Know?
What Have I LEARNED?

Are All Cells Alike?

All living things are made up of cells. Some organisms are composed of only one cell. Other organisms are made up of many cells.

1. What are the advantages of a one-celled organism?

2. What are the advantages of an organism that is made up of many cells?

7–1 Life Is Cellular

A. The Discovery of the Cell

  1. Early Microscopes

  2. The Cell Theory

B. Exploring the Cell

C. Prokaryotes and Eukaryotes

  1. Prokaryotes

  2. Eukaryotes

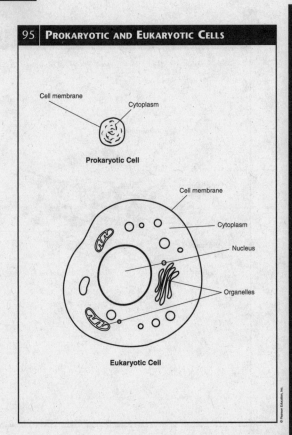

Prokaryotic Cell

Eukaryotic Cell

Division of Labor

A cell is made up of many parts with different functions that work together. Similarly, the parts of a computer work together to carry out different functions.

Working with a partner, answer the following questions.

1. What are some of the different parts of a computer? What are the functions of these computer parts?

2. How do the functions of these computer parts correspond to the functions of certain cell parts?

7–2 **Eukaryotic Cell Structure**

A. Comparing the Cell to a Factory

B. Nucleus

C. Ribosomes

D. Endoplasmic Reticulum

E. Golgi Apparatus

F. Lysosomes

G. Vacuoles

H. Mitochondria and Chloroplasts

   1. Mitochondria

   2. Chloroplasts

   3. Organelle DNA

I. Cytoskeleton

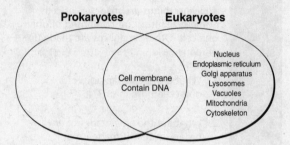

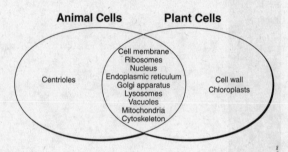

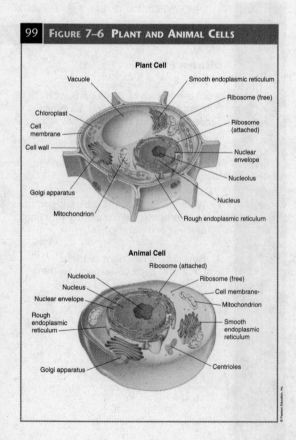

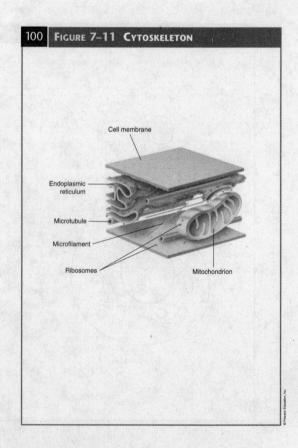

© Pearson Education, Inc., publishing as Pearson Prentice Hall.

In or Out?

How is a window screen similar to a cell membrane? Read on to find out.

1. What are some things that can pass through a window screen?

2. What are some things that cannot pass through a window screen? Why is it important to keep these things from moving through the screen?

3. The cell is surrounded by a cell membrane, which regulates what enters and leaves the cell. Why is it important to regulate what moves into and out of a cell?

7–3 Cell Boundaries

A. Cell Membrane

B. Cell Walls

C. Diffusion Through Cell Boundaries

    1. Measuring Concentration

    2. Diffusion

D. Osmosis

    1. How Osmosis Works

    2. Osmotic Pressure

E. Facilitated Diffusion

F. Active Transport

    1. Molecular Transport

    2. Endocytosis and Exocytosis

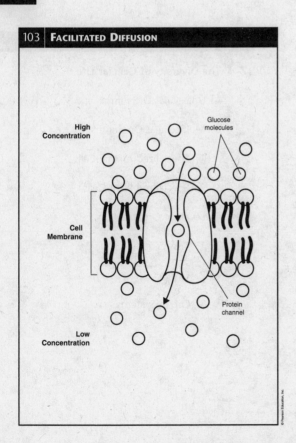

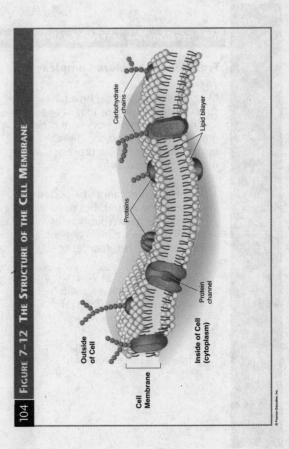

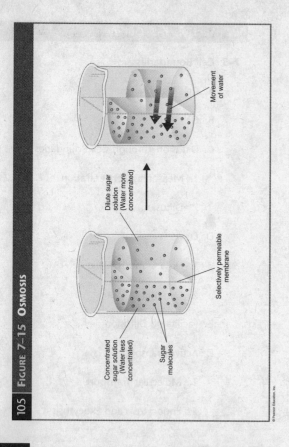

Dilute sugar solution (Water more concentrated)

Movement of water

Selectively permeable membrane

Concentrated sugar solution (Water less concentrated)

Sugar molecules

© Pearson Education, Inc.

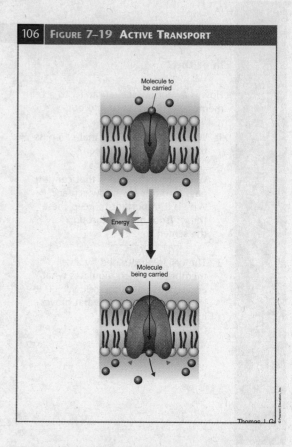

Molecule to be carried

Energy

Molecule being carried

© Pearson Education, Inc.

Thomas J. G

From Simple to More Complex

Many multicellular organisms have structures called organs that have a specific function and work with other organs. Working together, these organs carry out the life processes of the entire organism.

1. Some activities cannot be performed by only one person, but need a team of people. What type of activity requires a team of people to work together in order to complete a task?

2. What do you think are some characteristics of a successful team?

3. How is a multicellular organism similar to a successful team?

7–4 The Diversity of Cellular Life

A. Unicellular Organisms

B. Multicellular Organisms

  1. Specialized Animal Cells

  2. Specialized Plant Cells

C. Levels of Organization

  1. Tissues

  2. Organs

  3. Organ Systems

ANSWERS
1. Answers might include building a human pyramid or constructing an arch out of blocks.
2. Divide up jobs and cooperate well with one another
3. The functions of the organism are divided up among its parts (organs and organ systems). All the parts cooperate to carry out all the functions of the whole organism.

© Pearson Education, Inc.

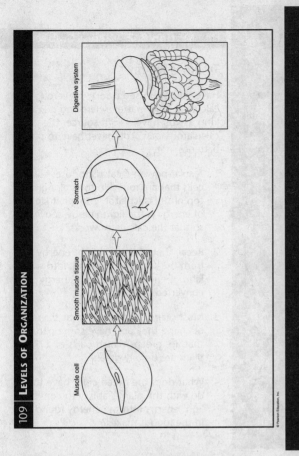

Digestive system

Stomach

Smooth muscle tissue

Muscle cell

Saving for a Rainy Day

Suppose you earned extra money by having a part-time job. At first, you might be tempted to spend all of the money, but then you decide to open a bank account.

1. What are the benefits of having a bank account?

2. What do you have to do if you need some of this money?

3. What might your body do when it has more energy than it needs to carry out its activities?

4. What does your body do when it needs energy?

ANSWERS
1. To save money and earn interest.
2. Go to the bank and take out the money you need.
3. Students will likely say that the body stores the energy.
4. Student answers may include that energy is gotten from food.

8–1 Energy and Life

A. Autotrophs and Heterotrophs

B. Chemical Energy and ATP

  1. Storing Energy

  2. Releasing Energy

C. Using Biochemical Energy

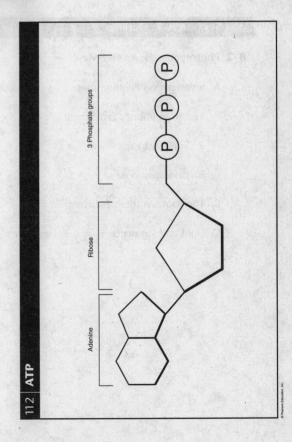

3 Phosphate groups

Ribose

Adenine

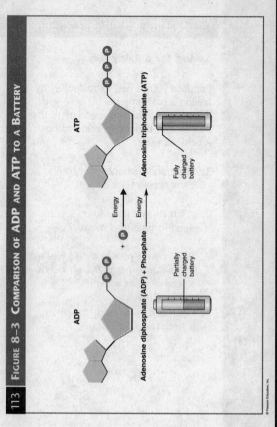

ATP

Adenosine triphosphate (ATP)

Fully charged battery

Energy

+ P

Energy

ADP

Adenosine diphosphate (ADP) + Phosphate

Partially charged battery

© Pearson Education, Inc.

Trapping Energy

Have you ever used a solar-powered calculator? No matter where you go, as long as you have a light source, the calculator works. You never have to put batteries in it.

1. A solar-powered calculator uses solar cells that are found in rows along the top of the calculator. Into what kind of energy is the light energy converted so that the calculator works?

2. Recall that plants use light energy from the sun to make food. Into what kind of energy is the light energy converted by plants?

3. Most plants, no matter what size or shape they are, have some parts that are green. Which parts of a plant are usually green?

4. What does the green color have to do with the plant's ability to convert light energy into the energy found in the food it makes?

ANSWERS
1. They convert light energy into electrical energy.
2. Plants convert light energy into chemical energy.
3. Leaves are green, as are some stems.
4. The green color is the pigment chlorophyll, which absorbs light energy from the sun and converts it to chemical energy in the process of photosynthesis.

© Pearson Education, Inc.

8–2 Photosynthesis: An Overview

A. Investigating Photosynthesis

   1. Van Helmont's Experiment

   2. Priestley's Experiment

   3. Jan Ingenhousz

B. The Photosynthesis Equation

C. Light and Pigments

© Pearson Education, Inc.

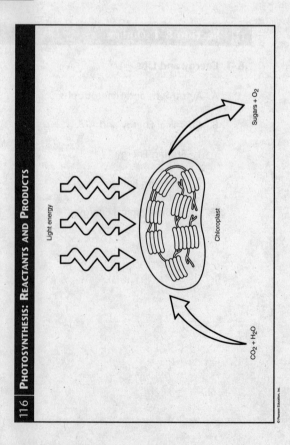

Light energy

Sugars + O_2

Chloroplast

$CO_2 + H_2O$

© Pearson Education, Inc.

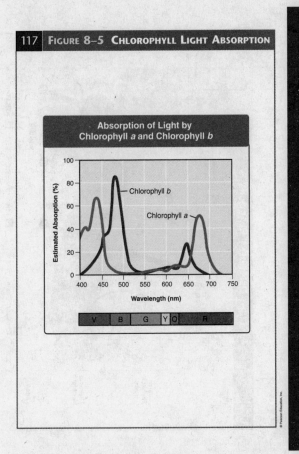

Absorption of Light by Chlorophyll *a* and Chlorophyll *b*

Chlorophyll *b*

Chlorophyll *a*

(y-axis) Estimated Absorption (%)
(x-axis) Wavelength (nm)

V B G Y O R

A Look Into the Future

It is 100 years in the future and you are a research scientist. An enormous volcanic eruption has recently sent huge quantities of dust and ash into the atmosphere.

Working with a partner, make a list of how this event will affect each of the following:

1. photosynthesis

2. plant life

3. animal life

4. human societies

ANSWERS
1. The rate of photosynthesis will decrease due to reduced sunlight. The rate of photosynthesis will decrease after a while due to fewer plants for herbivores and lower temperatures.
2. Plants will grow more slowly or die off due to decreased rate of photosynthesis.
3. Animal populations will decrease after a while due to fewer plants for herbivores and carnivores. The loss of plants will eventually result in fewer carnivores. Also, less oxygen will be available.
4. Human societies will have to adjust their eating habits as some food species die out.

8-3 The Reactions of Photosynthesis

A. Inside a Chloroplast

B. Electron Carriers

C. Light-Dependent Reactions

D. The Calvin Cycle

E. Factors Affecting Photosynthesis

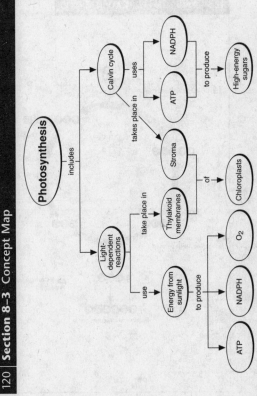

Photosynthesis
includes
Calvin cycle — uses — NADPH / ATP — to produce — High-energy sugars
takes place in — Stroma — of — Chloroplasts
Light-dependent reactions — take place in — Thylakoid membranes
Energy from sunlight — use — to produce — O₂ / NADPH / ATP

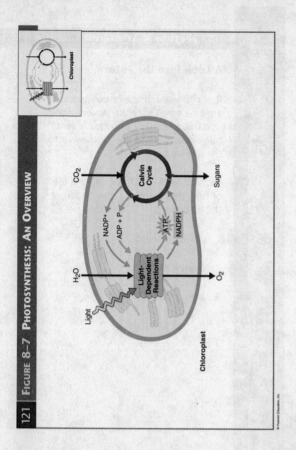

Chloroplast

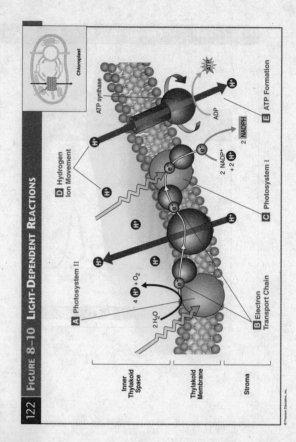

A Photosystem II
B Electron Transport Chain
C Photosystem I
D Hydrogen Ion Movement
E ATP Formation

ATP synthase

$4 H^+ + O_2$
$2 H_2O$
$2 NADP^+ + 2 H^+$
$2 NADPH$
ADP
ATP

Inner Thylakoid Space
Thylakoid Membrane
Stroma

Chloroplast

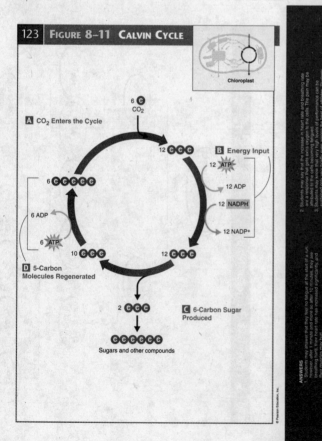

A CO$_2$ Enters the Cycle

6 C CO$_2$

12 CCC

B Energy Input

12 ATP
12 ADP
12 NADPH
12 NADP$^+$

6 CCCCC

6 ADP
6 ATP

D 5-Carbon Molecules Regenerated

10 CCC

12 CCC

2 CCC

C 6-Carbon Sugar Produced

CCCCCC

Sugars and other compounds

ANSWERS

1. Students may answer that they feel no fatigue at the start of a run; however, after 1 minute and more so after 10 minutes, they are breathing harder, their heart rate has increased significantly, and their muscles may hurt.

2. Students may say that the increase in heart rate and breathing rate are a response that delivers oxygen to the cells. This pace may be attributed to the cells becoming fatigued.

3. Students may know that very high levels of performance can be sustained only for a limited amount of time and distance. Students may say that the body runs out of readily available energy, food, or oxygen, so that the body builds up too many waste products in the cells.

Feel the Burn

Do you like to run, bike, or swim? These all are good ways to exercise. When you exercise, your body uses oxygen to get energy from glucose, a six-carbon sugar.

1. How does your body feel at the start of exercise, such as a long, slow run? How do you feel 1 minute into the run; 10 minutes into the run?

2. What do you think is happening in your cells to cause the changes in how you feel?

3. Think about running as fast as you can for 100 meters. Could you keep up this pace for a much longer distance? Explain your answer.

9–1 Chemical Pathways

A. Chemical Energy and Food

B. Overview of Cellular Respiration

C. Glycolysis

　1. ATP Production

　2. NADH Production

D. Fermentation

　1. Alcoholic Fermentation

　2. Lactic Acid Fermentation

126 | **CHEMICAL PATHWAYS**

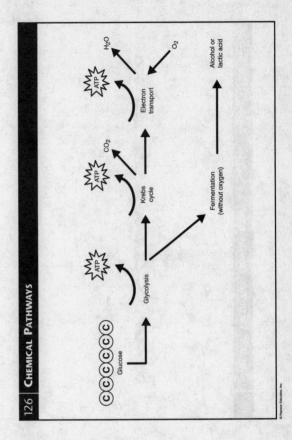

127 | **FIGURE 9–2 CELLULAR RESPIRATION: AN OVERVIEW**

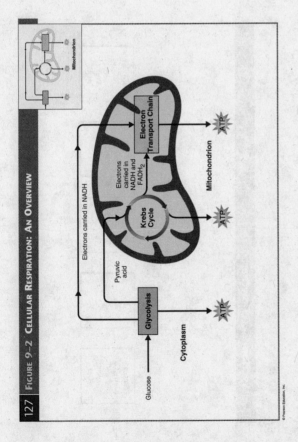

128 | **FIGURE 9–3 GLYCOLYSIS**

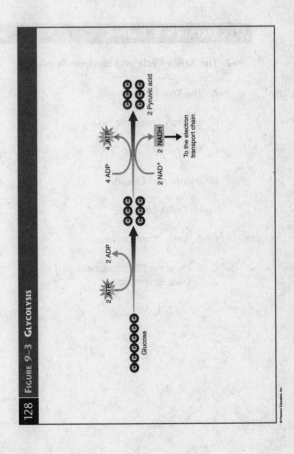

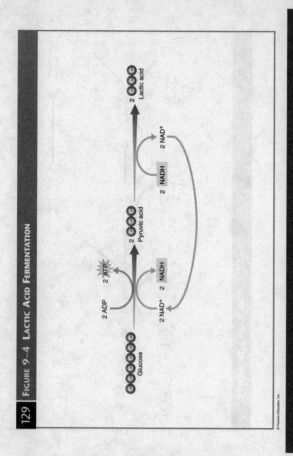

Glucose

2 ADP

2 ATP

2 NAD⁺ 2 NADH

Pyruvic acid

2 NAD⁺ 2 NADH

2 NAD⁺

Lactic acid

© Pearson Education, Inc.

Rolling and Folding

Some of the steps in cellular respiration take place in the membrane inside the cell structure called the mitochondrion, which has a folded inner membrane. What purpose do these folds serve?

To find out the answer to this question, perform this activity.

1. Obtain two sheets of paper and a metric ruler. What is the surface area of the paper?

2. Roll one sheet of paper into a tube lengthwise. What is the surface area of the rolled paper?

3. Fold the second sheet of paper into a fan. Then, roll the first sheet of paper around the folded paper so it is inside the rolled paper. What has happened to the surface area of the inside of the rolled paper?

4. What would be the value of increasing the surface area of the membrane inside a mitochondrion?

ANSWERS
1. The area will vary depending on the size of paper used. A sheet of notebook paper has an area of approximately 600 cm².
2. The surface area is the same as the surface area of the sheet of paper.
3. The surface area has increased (surface area of rolled paper + surface area of folded paper).
4. Increasing the surface area increases the amount of space where chemical reactions can take place.

© Pearson Education, Inc.

9-2 The Krebs Cycle and Electron Transport

A. The Krebs Cycle

B. Electron Transport

C. The Totals

D. Energy and Exercise

   1. Quick Energy

   2. Long-Term Energy

E. Comparing Photosynthesis and Cellular Respiration

© Pearson Education, Inc.

Cellular Respiration

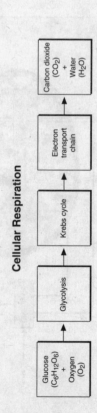

Glucose ($C_6H_{12}O_6$) + Oxygen (O_2)

Glycolysis

Krebs cycle

Electron transport chain

Carbon dioxide (CO_2) + Water (H_2O)

© Pearson Education, Inc.

Mitochondrion

Pyruvic acid

NAD⁺

NADH

CO₂

A Citric Acid Production

Acetyl-CoA

CoA

CoA
Coenzyme A

NADH

NAD⁺

Citric acid

CO₂

NAD⁺

NADH

FADH₂

FAD

B Energy Extraction

4-carbon compound

5-carbon compound

ADP

ATP

NADH

NAD⁺

CO₂

© Pearson Education, Inc.

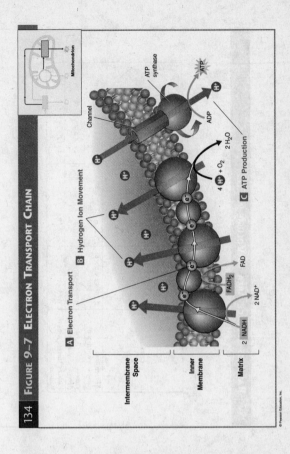

Mitochondrion

ATP synthase

ATP

Channel

H⁺

ADP

2 H₂O

4 H⁺ + O₂

C ATP Production

B Hydrogen Ion Movement

FAD

FADH₂

2 NAD⁺

2 NADH

A Electron Transport

Intermembrane Space

Inner Membrane

Matrix

© Pearson Education, Inc.

Getting Through

Materials move through cells by diffusion. Oxygen and food move into cells, while waste products move out of cells. How does the size of a cell affect how efficiently materials get to all parts of a cell?

Work with a partner to complete this activity.

1. On a sheet of paper, make a drawing of a cell that has the following dimensions: 5 cm x 5 cm x 5 cm. Your partner should draw another cell about one half the size of your cell on a separate sheet of paper.

2. Compare your drawings. How much longer do you think it would take to get from the cell membrane to the center of the big cell than from the cell membrane to the center of the smaller cell?

3. What is the advantage of cells being small?

ANSWERS
2. It would take twice the amount of time.
3. If cells are small, materials can be distributed to all parts of the cell quickly.

10–1 Cell Growth

A. Limits to Cell Growth

1. DNA "Overload"

2. Exchanging Materials

3. Ratio of Surface Area to Volume

4. Cell Division

© Pearson Education, Inc.

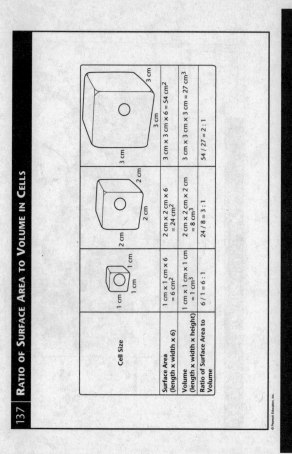

Cell Size	1 cm cube	2 cm cube	3 cm cube
Surface Area (length × width × 6)	1 cm × 1 cm × 6 = 6 cm²	2 cm × 2 cm × 6 = 24 cm²	3 cm × 3 cm × 6 = 54 cm²
Volume (length × width × height)	1 cm × 1 cm × 1 cm = 1 cm³	2 cm × 2 cm × 2 cm = 8 cm³	3 cm × 3 cm × 3 cm = 27 cm³
Ratio of Surface Area to Volume	6 / 1 = 6 : 1	24 / 8 = 3 : 1	54 / 27 = 2 : 1

© Pearson Education, Inc.

Cell Cycle

The cell cycle represents recurring events that take place in the period of time from the beginning of one cell division to the beginning of the next. In addition to cell division, the cell cycle includes periods when the cell is growing and actively producing materials it needs for the next division.

1. Why is the cell cycle called a cycle?

2. Why do you think that it is important for a cell to grow in size during its cell cycle?

3. What might happen to a cell if all events leading up to cell division took place as they should, but the cell did not divide?

ANSWERS
1. It represents recurring events.
2. If a cell did not grow in size, each cell division would produce progressively smaller cells.
3. Students may infer that a cell that undergoes all sequences of the cell cycle should grow and divide. To continue to grow, while the cell could no longer exchange materials with the environment efficiently enough to live.

© Pearson Education, Inc.

10–2 Cell Division

A. Chromosomes

B. The Cell Cycle

C. Events of the Cell Cycle

D. Mitosis

   1. Prophase

   2. Metaphase

   3. Anaphase

   4. Telophase

E. Cytokinesis

© Pearson Education, Inc.

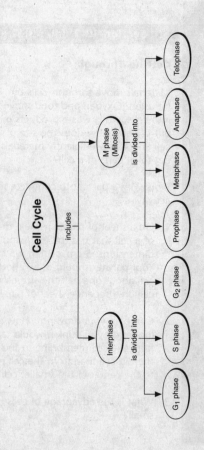

© Pearson Education, Inc.

DNA replication

S phase

Interphase

G₁ phase

Cell growth

Cell division

Cytokinesis
Telophase
Anaphase
Metaphase
Prophase

Mitosis

M phase

Preparation for mitosis

G₂ phase

© Pearson Education, Inc.

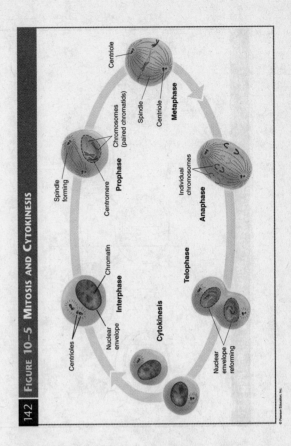

Centriole

Spindle

Centriole

Metaphase

Chromosomes (paired chromatids)

Prophase

Spindle forming

Centromere

Individual chromosomes

Anaphase

Chromatin

Interphase

Centrioles

Nuclear envelope

Telophase

Cytokinesis

Nuclear envelope reforming

© Pearson Education, Inc.

Knowing When to Stop

Suppose you had a paper cut on your finger. Although the cut may have bled and stung a little, after a few days, it will have disappeared, and your finger would be as good as new.

1. How do you think the body repairs an injury, such as a cut on a finger?

2. How long do you think this repair process continues?

3. What do you think causes the cells to stop the repair process?

ANSWERS
1. The cut is repaired by the production of new cells through cell division.
2. Cell division continues until the cut is replaced.
3. Students will likely say that when the cut is filled in, there is no room for more cells to grow.

© Pearson Education, Inc.

10–3 Regulating the Cell Cycle

A. Controls on Cell Division

B. Cell Cycle Regulators

   1. Internal Regulators

   2. External Regulators

C. Uncontrolled Cell Growth

© Pearson Education, Inc.

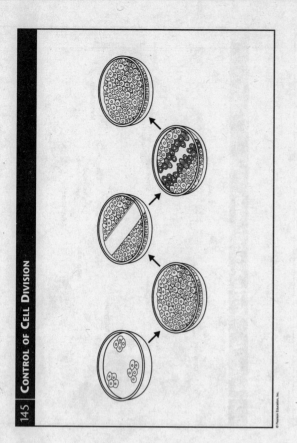

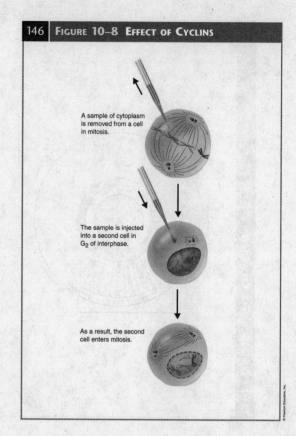

A sample of cytoplasm is removed from a cell in mitosis.

The sample is injected into a second cell in G_2 of interphase.

As a result, the second cell enters mitosis.